You cannot choose
Your teachers......

You cannot choose Your teachers......
Some learned, unlearned or rejected….

Jayashree

Interior Illustrations by Seema Taneja

PARTRIDGE

To order additional copies of this book, contact
Partridge India
000 800 10062 62
orders.india@partridgepublishing.com

www.partridgepublishing.com/india

Contents

Am I A Happy Woman?

Am I better off than my grandma?
In many ways, "YES"!.

Well, I managed to get out of my house, got education, worked (read economic independence) and I use superior technology.

Now, the second question:

Am I happier than my Grandma?
Hmm....here is the catch. I believe that in spite of all the advantages I have, she was happier than me.

Her world was smaller, her information and needs were lesser. Yet she was happy; I mean happier than me. Today I have a world of opportunity she could not have even dreamt of yet she who lived in a remote village with almost no connectivity, was way happier than me.

I have a problem with this advocacy of equality of sexes. I feel that the entire concept of women's' liberation, empowerment etc. have been coined by some very chauvinistic male. One that makes me scream is – **multitasking**. I have seen a lot of my peers including me caught in the tyranny of multitasking. This word means a woman pursues a career and does the classic balancing act of managing the home front too while the men after giving the mandatory hours to a career, happily procrastinate.

Another such term is blurring gender roles. I read a lot of articles where they talk about "blurring lines" of roles meant for men and women. I agree the lines have not just blurred they have even vanished for some women, but what about the Adam family? Well they still live in Eden, which means, once their working hours are over, they have unquestioned control over the remote, vanish for all boys' parties, sports and events, etc. There are exceptions of course, there is a new breed called the metro sexual male who will don an apron once in a blue moon to "unwind" and cook something as it is a "stress buster", mind you the metro female is expected to swoon with delight over the "sensitivity" and then march into the kitchen to clean up the mess; after all she is a multitasking woman.

With so much noise about women empowerment one issue that has been in limelight is women being allowed in temples even while they menstruate. I am remember my mother saying how much she loved those days of menstrual confinement; yummy food, and no chores. Ask yourselves women, if you had your way, would you not have had those four days given to you as a holiday from ALL? And here are some women who want even that respite to be taken away!

By saying this, I am not propagating the purdah and medieval mind set. I have a matriarchal ancestry with women having more shares of property than males. That was a system where men stayed at their wife's home. My women ancestors were far more liberal than and broadminded than me or a woman today. In the face of a disagreement, men would leave the home and it was not out of order for men to have more than one family. Under those circumstances, the women never hesitated to give the wayward husband the boot but accepted his children who participated in all family functions as one of their own.

I wonder how many liberal women of this sort are there today.

Not me for sure!

So, on this Woman's day, I wonder am I better off than my grandma or her mom?

Perhaps Khalil Gibran is right!

"Modern civilization has made woman a little wiser, but it has increased her suffering because of man's covetousness. The woman of yesterday was a happy wife, but the woman of today is a miserable mistress. In the past she walked blindly in the light, but now she walks open-eyed in the dark. She was beautiful in her ignorance, virtuous in her simplicity, and strong in her weakness. Today she has become ugly in her ingenuity, superficial and heartless in her knowledge. Will the day ever come when beauty and knowledge, ingenuity and virtue, and weakness of body and strength of spirit will be united in a woman?"

On Buying A Walking Stick.......

"Get me a walking stick" said my 83 year old mother; First as a reaction and then a plea.

It is not easy to see parents grow old.

I lost my father when he was still young, strong and dynamic. Even time could not fill that vacuum. So, his memory lives on guiding me, sometimes by appearing in my dreams to never give up and take difficult and unpleasant decisions. He lives in me and I reflect him in my actions. That is how I came to terms with losing my father.

I never saw my father weak and infirm. Short with an athletic built he could have put any "gym" frequenting youngster to shame. In many ways a paradox; with an almost "my way or the highway" attitude, he was incredibly caring and sensitive He was someone whom friends and family loved, feared and looked up to. So, when he left us, I carried this image in my mind and he is my role model.

My mother and I, like most mother daughter duos have had our shares of fights, disagreements and yet a strong womanly bond that makes us understand each other like nobody else can. As a working woman, her financial independence along with exposure made her a fun companion, particularly in my teens. Since she worked with the USSR information Centre, for her it was routine to meet stalwarts like Aruna Asaf Ali, Harivanshrai Bachchan, Habib Tanveer, Kaifi Azmi, Bhisham Sahani (whose wife was also her colleague). She had passes to most cultural events in Delhi of National and International importance. So, I grew up watching plays, listening to music maestros and dance performances by almost all icons of classical dancing. I even had the fortune to watch an excerpt of the ***swan lake*** and shake hands with the performers of Bolshoi theatre.

Her office was at 25 Barakhamba Road. So, Connaught Place, Janpath and Shankar Market were a routine haunt for us. There is no shop there where we have not bought something, no food that we have not sampled. For many years, after leaving Delhi, I still would postpone all my shopping to holidays when I would visit Delhi.

From a small cosy village in Kozhikode, Kerala, she had come a long way. It seems when my father's marriage proposal came to my mother's family, they did not want to marry their daughter to a man who worked in some strange land- Delhi. But my mother was all excited....an an avid reader, this was an opportunity for her to see and experience all that she had read. Even without seeing my father, she had prayed that this should be the man in her life. My mother says she had no sorrow or regret about leaving her village. She took to Delhi like fish to water. My father, one of the founding members of the Delhi Malayalee Association and the Admin Head of USSR Information Center, was like a jewel in the crown, whetting her appetite to interact with more and more celebrities; about people she had read about but never dreamt of meeting face to face.

A woman who literally had wheels on her feet, asked me for a walking stick! I can imagine how helpless she must feel to ask me for a support. As it is she feels guilty to see me stay home, leaving my work to tend to her and this walking stick is like a symbol of ultimate dependence. I humour her, I tell her that she has become empowered to hit us once again, but somewhere the laugh is not coming from my heart. It sounds hollow and contrived. Today she is hard of hearing, wheezes and walks with effort. Every day, I see her weakening, slowly slipping away. The only time I see her old self is when she reads or when she watches a ***Bajrangi Bhaijaan*** with moist eyes, carrying the kid on his shoulders to a strange land, with strange people.....

Beatle Mania

I the super mom!

I the perfect wife!

And the very people around whom my existence revolves FORGOT my birthday????????!!!!!!!!!!!!!!!!!!!!!!!!!!

This was the most unimaginable, the very pinnacle of ego bashing that I could take. While my husband and my elder son tip toed around me knowing that any move or gesture from them could spark an explosion, my younger one did the impossible.

I entered my home at night to see a huge poster of "The BEATLES" spread out with a "BEATLES" cup and a "BEATLES" fridge sticker. Note- the poster was black and white.

The best balm to a broken heart is perhaps to revive and touch a teenage crush. My son did just that. I sat down and made the first call of the day to my family- my son to tell him how much I loved the poster. It is not as if my elder son is not aware of my crush, I still carry the "Beatles" clutch that he had got for me from London, but my younger one knew exactly when to touch that craze.

So, the poster had to be framed and displayed. Off I went to a nearby shop and displayed the poster and some other pictures of Pt Ravi Shankar and George Harrison (All in black and white) to be framed. The shop keeper too looked at my "weird" choice of getting a poster which has four gangly boys walking down a street in an austere black frame compared to Gods and Goddesses of all religions in gold gilded frames. He must have attributed my choice to vanishing sanity, a natural phenomenon at my age!

I went to check the poster and was glad to see that he had done a good job. I saw a man wearing the uniform of a guard in the shop. He left the moment I entered the shop. Having inspected the pictures, I stepped into the ATM next door to withdraw some money and almost jumped out of my skin to hear a voice ask, "Madam, where did you get that Beatles poster from?"

I turned to see the security guard in the photo frame shop sitting inside the ATM. I told him it is a gift from my son. He went on to discuss the songs of BEATLES and also some other "Indian born singers" like Cliff Richard and Engle Herbert Humperdinck. I heard him with wonder and realised that we both share the same craze and passion for music. He talked at length about the songs sung by BEATLES; the mastery of Ringo Starr on the guitar and the experimentation of George Harrison. In that tiny cubicle we talked about how The BEATLES changed our lives. Changed what we laughed about, changed how we felt, changed how we

Ruben Issac, my music pal retired from Bosch and is now working as a security guard. He is as faceless as all of us who live in big cities but his love for music gave him a face, an identity. In perspective I could understand and justify my indignation and hurt after all it questioned the basis of my identity.

But it also made one thing very clear; there are somethings deep within my core which cannot be shaken by social bindings, which is above relationships which is totally, unabashedly, selfishly ME.

In this case- BEATLE MANIA.

Boys Will Be Boys!

Doston se bichadkar yeh haqeqat khuli Galib
Kamine to bahut the, magar raunak unhi se thi

It was an almost maniac ranting.....let's go to **Jabalpur**, I want to drive in the jungles, I want to roam in <u>Sadar</u>, I want to cast a line in *Narmada*...

For a city bred impersonal me, this obsession was beyond comprehension. I can understand having a soft corner for places where you have spent your growing years but an obsession? As a Delhiite, I miss Delhi no doubt but I certainly am NOT obsessed with Connaught Place, Janpath, Palika Bazar, Karol Bagh, Tip Dabs, Kamla Nagar, Lajpat Nagar, Sarojini Nagar, Def Col, etc etc etc.........

So, I tried everything in my power to dissuade- logic- illogic; religion-atheism; practicality- emotion ...anything to get this obsession off. Then I used my most potent weapon, my Agni missile- "I cannot come" again with logic, illogic, religion, atheism, practicality, emotion...but to my utter horror it failed. Not just that it failed, it failed completely. I could not even alter the plan- i.e. driving 1,365 Km. Well, my credibility as a wife was now at stake. So, out came my Bhramastra- "you don't care how worried I will be if you drive". I suppose I pushed too far as I got a painful response- "okay, I won't go". Now like any self-respecting wife a helpless, surrendering husband is just not acceptable! Can you imagine how uneventful and dreadfully boring marriage will become if the zest of a confrontation just fizzles out??!!. It really gave me the shuderrrrrrrrsssssss and so with the intuitive wisdom of a woman I realized that this is the time to let go.

So, off he sped even before the sun, well stocked (long drives can make you oh so thirsty!); every stop neatly planned. Updates about the condition of the road, weather, people, eateries kept reaching me till the destination- Jabalpur.

Once there- the three musketeers united. They ate when they wanted, drank when they felt like, swam and splashed around like boys and drove around the city till crazy. In 15 days, they relived their childhood haunts and even rivalries going to an extent of demanding the same medication given to one of them just to keep the spoils and privileges fair and square. Sometimes when I would interrupt this reverie with a call, I heard boyish, boisterous laughter interrupted with accounts of squabbles such as "he stole my marbles"

They cheated to get better of each other by having an extra *aloo bonda*, an extra helping of fish, one more bite of juicy farm fresh chicken and an extra peg of booze. Like teenagers they argued on their conquests over fairer sex no matter how they are today, they fought over a heavy leg, snores and farts forgetting their receding hairlines and white overtaking grey.

All of them into their fifties, successful, settled, happy and content, they parted only with a promise to meet again. This journey, this getaway was really important. It connected them to those feelings when they loved, laughed, cried and cursed as teenagers. This experience touched something deep within. It revived and relived an experience no expensive or exotic vacation could have given; it touched the freshness and effervescence of boyhood.

Jai Sri Ram!

Call it a fall out of deep rooted conditioning, a result of etched images created by the sonorous voice of a warm and cosy Grandma.

Call it a fall out of upbringing, where even a casual greeting or an exclamation for all emotions echo "Ram"

Call it the fall out of a reformed feminist who saw the strength of Seeta, the devoted wife

Call it the fall out of acquaintances that have made religion (read conversion) a lucrative business

Call it the admission of an apologist Hindu, thanks to a politically engineered education system

........I experienced the divine. I was overwhelmed and silenced. Every pore in me sang in adulation of the power; the power of elements that whirled around me; the power of the divine.

The moment I set foot on the bridge that connected the Pamban Island to India; I knew that the place was special. No. I was not a typical tourist taken in by the sight of a huge expanse of eater especially when I had lived by a sea for almost 4 years. But this was different. When I stood on the bridge, it was not just my hair that whirled, it was my entire being.

11

Like a typical professional, I dismissed it to the feeling of a person who spends most waking hours cut off from elements in a controlled, sanitized, noise free environment. But, the best was yet to come. I set off to *Dhanushkodi* and the feeling came back, with renewed force and energy. The rickety drive over the sea bed to the edge of the sea at *Dhanushkodi*, was an experience in itself. Standing at the shore with Bay of Bengal on my left and the Indian ocean on my right, I could feel how blessed I am to stand on that land. The blinding, deafening breeze, the whirling sand, the sheer power of nature filled me with awe and reverence for the MAN who conquered it all.

The village of ***Dhanushkodi,*** now a ghost village, after the 1964 cyclone. This village has very little people living in it. I saw the remains of a church, a railway station and a railway colony set by the British destroyed after the 1964 cyclone. In one hut there was a make shift temple and they had a stone of the famed ***Ram Setu***. There was a cement trough that would have about two buckets of water. A stone- The Stone floated in that trough in just about two buckets of water.

The sceptic in me challenged and prodded my faith once again. I put my hand in and tried to lift the stone- it would not budge; such was the weight. Yet it floated. That Ghost village on the sea bed had fresh water at depth of 2-3 feet! The villager told us that one could get fresh water even if you dig the sand with bare hands along the line of Ram Setu. The sceptic again screamed "impossible" and dismissed the faith of the villager. So, I tasted the water, ah! sweet it was! I was told that the temple in Rameshwaram has wells with fresh water; but this was even further in the sea...20 km. further into the sea!

Since Google God has a lot of say in my beliefs today, I turned to my Google and returned with no answers. What was the stone made of? How could such a heavy stone float in such little water? How can there be sweet water on a land almost on the sea bed?

Back in Bangalore, I wondered why I questioned this experience.

Why did I need to search for evidence?

Why did I need to reason my experience?

Why did I need to deny my experience?

Why was I ashamed of articulating what I experienced?

Why do I hesitate to articulate my experience without a pang of guilt?

Why do I fear that my experience will be dismissed as a figment of imagination?

Why do I, an Indian, a Hindu have to make an excuse to acknowledge my faith to myself?

Why should I forgive my education, my social conditioning; the wily politicians who have taken away the comfort and security of my Faith from me?

This write up is in response to Liquor Prohibition in Kerala which has the notoriety of being the state with largest consumption of liquor in India.

Mallu Without Madhyam!!!!!!!!

Oh! Woe befall this God's own country!
What is a true blue blooded Mallu
Without his Mund and Meesha
Without his Kappa and Meen curry
Without his bar and his "small s"

Prohibition? At a time when Mahabali is due for his annual visit? How ill-timed could this decision have been! The "zing" out of Onam is gone. All a Mallu can think of is- 2015 as the year of the Doomsday, the day of Judgement.

The tremor of this news was felt even in Bangalore, my on-road companion was so disoriented that he missed a turn on the road, a turn he had been taking for so long that it was genetically coded in him. Even in the metro, the usual Mallu guys were missing- perhaps they would have boarded later train- news like this hits one hard and takes time to sink in! I am sure every Mallu world over must be completely shocked.....what is the point of their slogging, far away from their homeland when they can't go for a holiday to "Naadu", sit under the shade of the evening sky, with coconut trees, and music of water lapping the shores and get drunk with "kootkars"

Anybody who has visited Kerala even as a wide eyed tourist will agree that Mallus are well behaved and proud people. The best example of their good behaviour is the patience with which they queue up outside liquor shops every morning without fail. They strongly believe in the concept of work life balance. Whatever profession a Mallu is involved in, irrespective of the hours of work; come evening and he can be spotted in a "Kallu Shaapp" or a "Bar" depending on his economic status. Sunset in Kerala is the beginning of happiness and all around we see happy people only getting argumentative if you question the global impact Che Guevara, Fidel Castro, Chavez, etc

If the people are drinking and are happy about it, what is the Govt's problem? All those religious leaders are worried that people will not turn to them for solutions. Religion has always been a powerful intoxicant; so the issue is that people have found an alternative exclusive of these agents of God. If a man can drown and forget his woes of existence with a couple of pegs, then who will turn to those agents of God? They are going out of business hence this hue and cry.

Besides, logic says that people drink a lot because they like that "SPIRITual" state. If this is taken away what will they do? They will either start brewing at home of turn to other forms of intoxication. Man needs a break from the cruelty of routine and mundane existence that is why forms of intoxication existed in earliest of civilizations, some of them even attributed it to Gods called it Soma or Somaras. Besides, in a democracy why should the government interfere with what people like to eat and drink? An adult must have this freedom of choice. Why is the Govt. not governing? Why are they donning the mantle of a moral police?

In fact it is time for the Government to introspect and wonder why there is such a huge consumption of liquor in Kerala; the most literate state with a decent development index. When people turn to intoxication there is a trigger. Without addressing the cause, the Govt has decided to pull out the antidote. Hence the cause remains.....and it's just a matter of time when a fertile Mallu brain comes up with an elevating solution

India is a land of multiple languages. The ability to communicate in English is limited to a miniscule population in India. This write up is in response to the government's move to make English the medium of writing examinations

What Is An Indian
Who Knows No English?

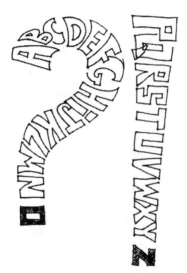

This write up would be a little ironical as proficiency in English language happens to be my bread and butter. But, my experience while interacting with students almost all over India, has led to a belief that ability to communicate in English has nothing much to do with a students' calibre or other qualities like leadership, creativity etc.

Years of my career in teaching English has seen a breed of colleagues (Teachers of English) whose knowledge or information remains trapped within the first and the last page of the text book. Some of these "English Teachers" (literally) are "convented" while some come from a family where Pidgin English is their mother tongue. Most of them are usually clueless about the beauty and versatility of English as a language that has encompassed the various cultures of the world in its proud imperious march over the globe. They are rarely updated about new writing in English and sadly many whom I know do not even read the newspaper. Such is the impact of English that a lot of them even put on accents and behave as if they were unfortunate to be left teaching English in India. They resolutely refuse to acknowledge Indian writers in English as English is all about fair skin and British.

Compare this with a regional language teacher. Here the teacher has the advantage of a much richer and relevant literature that connects well with the socio- economic background of the student. The teacher does not have to struggle to teach a foreign language. The teacher has the freedom to expose the students to the way people have used words to capture every complex feeling. The teacher can inspire the students to dream and aspire to make their lives more happy and meaningful. But just take a look at this teacher; where is the pride; where is the confidence; what makes them look such poor cousins to the "I know it all" looking "English teachers"?. Why do they need to look a pathetic image of a humility and meekness?

When I switched my career to Training again due to the onus of English language and the BPO boom, I was in for a bigger shock. Here were handpicked engineers being trained to speak English with the right roll of the "r" and curl of the "l" by people who were nowhere close to them in education or competence. Today the Training industry has a huge breed of people with a great love for their voices but scant subject knowledge. Some of them even mimic the air hostesses who speak both English and Hindi with a weird incomprehensible accent. But the sad fact is that they thrive as they have a captive audience, thanks to the politicization of education.

I am in full support of the students who have managed to make the government bend to their demands of not making English compulsory while writing the exams. When the government has done nothing to promote English as a link language in a country with such diverse tongues like India, then what right do they have to impose this language as a filter for deserving candidates?

In fact this language English alone is responsible for a new kind of a caste or creed of students. On one hand we have students in big cities that have become so internationally aware that they have begun to celebrate Halloween but do not know the difference between Independence Day and Republic Day. And on the other we have students who go study without even a proper school and compete with their privileged counterparts in big cities with success.

Till the government streamlines the education delivered in all schools with at least 70% uniformity, let them not dare to interfere with the opportunities for which a student has struggled with no help let alone encouragement.

A Salute To Life

Kaanton se kheench key yeh aanchal
Tod ke bandhan baandhi paayal
Koi na roke dil ki udaan ko
Dil who chala............

I have not stopped humming these lines since yesterday....since I met you, Mridula. Through the bus ride back home, through the treacherous traffic, at night when I put down my head to rest, in the morning with surya namaskar, now sitting in office.......I can't but marvel at the way you have transformed. The way you have come out of that cage, built by you and by destiny, you have broken it all and come out free.....a beautiful butterfly, full of colours of life, radiating joy in every breath, an example of celebration of life!

There were times when I wondered and even resented the way you would give in so easily. The way people doubted your ability, the way people manipulated you, the way people ran you down..........and it was more frustrating that you knew it all and yet you suffered and ignored. When destiny struck you a mighty blow....I watched stunned and I saw you crumble in its tyranny. I wondered at the fairness of karma and could not comprehend why you were chosen to be smothered, suffocated from all sides.

But seeing you now, it explains all. You have defeated them all. And what is more, you have grown wings and like the proverbial Icarus you will not burn yourself anymore. You have already taken off and now you hover above all of us, watching us, smiling at us, still loving us with your characteristic indulgence.

Even after all this I am amazed that you value relationships. You have no rancour against the people who left you in your moment of need. You have shrugged away the hurt, dismissed it to their weakness and have decided to move on......and trust me move on you will.

Yesterday, you looked radiant, in bright colours. While you took a call from a client, I watched with awe how much of a power you are to reckon with. You negotiated and transacted with such élan that I gaped... Completely exorcised of those relationships that weighed you and a disease that threatened your existence, you stand confident and tall, untouched, unaffected and serene.

Though I have taught a lot from you Mridula, the most important thing you have taught me is how wonderful the world is and how beautiful life is! I thank my destiny today that I was fortunate to be a part of your lifetime!

Life In A Metro

"What is this life if, full of care,
We have no time to stand and stare"

William Wordsworth

I think about these lines at least twice a day. Now that I have begun to commute by public transport, my mind and body free from manoeuvring the impossible Bangalore traffic, I in all earnestness take time out to stare. But I am shocked at my co commuters......They get into the tube mechanically and alight robot-like completely oblivious to life moving all around them.

The greatest culprit here is those mobile phones or better still a smart phone. There is a huge population out there that is wired in. They have ear plugs firmly in their ears and their smart phones to which they hold on to, dearer than their lives. There are many who pull out their mobiles and glance and even scroll any stored information on it just to belong to that breed of cell phone addicts. There are some who pull out a book, particularly the life style, Robin Sharma kind of books and read without a page turning for weeks at a stretch. Can't blame them as the metro ride is short and by the time they get the hang of where they left last in the book, it's time to get off. Then comes the breed of really busy bodies who work so hard in office that they catch up with all the office gossip. The insight that I have of their complex personalities is something even their mothers are clueless of. Then there are the fashionistas who soak in the admiring and envious looks with an impassive distant unseeing look.

My young travel companion and I have consciously decided to make the best of this journey by talking and staring at all that our eyes can take. Since the metro is elevated to the level of a tree line, we watch the greenery soaking in the sunshine in the morning, dancing in the mild tea time Bangalore drizzle and swaying to the breeze, the houses that race by us with their beautifully laid out balconies with flower pots and plants, the harsh concrete structures that have replaced the trees that was once a symbol of this garden city. Between all those buildings are the colourful temples with their painted yakshas watching the world that has overtaken all their power. We chat about people who have taken the road less travelled by travelling the world by road, about travellers we read in books who travelled a life time to just watch and stare at the wonder called the earth and the even more wonderful creature called MAN

As I consciously fight my desire to belong, to race with the teeming crowd, I make the guard at the metro uncomfortable. He cannot understand why I let the train go by without rushing in to board it. He looks at me, blows his whistle as if saying, "Move on woman....don't slow down......don't stop". And all I do is stare at him, tribal features in a guard's uniform, smooth dark skin, eyes questioning, eyes shining and face full of wonder, bony with remnants of teenage in his boyish eyes

The Missing Bits

Small things are really big and they matter and matter a lot at that. Maybe a chauvinist attitude would dismiss it as an existential fall out of living in the misty world of Mills and Boon. Yet it is these small things that make a person feel what everybody is – unique.

All of us cherish that uniqueness that sets us apart from others. When we share a life with someone or some people that core still remains as it is Untouched, unmoved and strictly personal-ME. That uniqueness that sets us apart objectively must never be ignored or compromised on. The travails of existence sometimes take its toll when these small things are passed over and ignored. And as a woman these little things mean a world. Maybe, women are more sensitive about those little things, hence they take care that the little things are never missed by those for whom they care. These little somethings are rarely noticed but when missed, it is painfully evident. Imagine a life without these little things-. A gentle fleeting touch oozing with affection, the extra mile in teeming traffic to pick that specific thing that matters, the hours spent in setting up a comfort, the minutes that run into hours for casual routine call only to assure that you are safe. Well men might just dismiss this as the musings of a head in the clouds romantic.

Romance has been synonymous with the vulnerable and nubile, female species who turn to the broad shoulders of a man for succour; a thought perpetrated by man who throws tit bits of indulgence towards a woman when he is in good humour. If not he turns insensitive and stone like a quintessential macho. Hence the picture of a strong man is always impassive, his arms are usually crossed challengingly and seems to look into a distant horizon. No room for emotion here. No room for tenderness; just strong and distant. Any display contrary to that is "moments of weakness" That is why a woman's tenderness and surrender is always a sign of weakness. A happy ending always has a woman surrendering even being grateful to the hard-hearted man who showers divine blessing on the woman by sacrificing his independence to be her saviour forever and ever....till death does them apart!

But then what about a woman who defies the image of a typical romantic? What about a woman who has strong- mind, body and heart? What about a woman who seeks a friend in a man? Does it mean that she has gone beyond those little things that make her feel like a woman? Does it mean that all those little things can be given a pass over? Does it mean that she exists and does not even deserve the civility that is reserved even for casual acquaintances?

A woman too has a little "self" beyond the roles that she plays. That self only craves for that little "bit" which has been passed over or been taken for granted. That missing 'bit' ignored again and again leading to a vacuum that nothing can or will fill. Draupadi, a woman who was denied childhood, sought love in the valour of the world's best archer, and the bit in her was crushed time and again- when she had to share her love, when she had to welcome another woman and the culmination when her mighty husbands became mute spectators to her public disrobement; no amount of valour on the battle field could fill those missing bits which when denied left a black hole full of sorrow and bitterness. The vacuum that Sita felt when she had to take the test of fire; no matter her husband vanquished the mightiest, but that test, a moment of truth, threw light on that glaring missing bit.

That bit of the "self" demands no gifts, no diamonds but yes if not tended the "rust" is bound to set in.

Pride In Being A Woman

Why is there a special day dedicated to a woman?

Is it that she is remembered on this day and rest of the days belong to men?

Is it an attempt to create a cult or a group? If so; to what end?

The very fact that we all recognize a day as the "Women's' day "is also a tacit surrender or recognition that rest of the days belong to men. With the power of 49 being touted by the media and the social media with an almost militant intensity, I can't help but wonder if this is an acknowledgement of the power of men.

A woman needs to recognize herself as an individual and that too without a tom-tom to proclaim the qualities that nature has by design endowed her with. The day she demands or craves approval or attention that too for her femininity, she gives another booster shot to the male dominance emotional or physical.

A study of the increasing atrocities against women leads mostly to one relevant point- absence of a self- respecting woman in their lives. The much celebrated movies like **Mother India** and the more recent **Godmother** proves that a family which has a woman who respects herself commands respect from males too. Strangely, this internal empowerment has nothing much to do with education. My grandmothers, confined to their homes and villages were way stronger than me. They went through the vicissitudes of life without losing their dignity; in every sense a perfect companion to their husbands. Even closer, my mother, otherwise a quiet and meek person, surprises me with her objectivity and I remember my dynamic hands –on father, always respected her views without a question.

It's not as if my mother had it easy for her. In spite of her brilliance in school, she was never allowed to continue with her studies as it would mean leaving her village. So, she became a learner for life. Her sheer brilliance earned her a job and worked illustriously till retirement. All this while, she was a perfect foil for my socially ambitious father. Right from being a proactive support to his almost decaying family, she was the quiet strength behind all his ventures and endeavours. She was rarely heard or even seen but it was evident that she was his strength. Even after I lost my father, she continued to be an anchor. Though she prefers the company of books to anything else, she is always there for me

As a child she wanted me to study and learn everything that could be taught- music, dance, horse riding, swimming, driving along with formal education. Socially she taught me to forget and forgive and that it is not a sign of weakness, that we have to take the lead to build bridges. She taught me that it is undignified to parade myself as a commodity and to never use my "female" status to any advantage.

Today I can say proudly that I am a woman and I celebrate it every living moment.

The Pumpkin Of Contention

In many ways, the housing society I stay in mirrors the nation more so now when the pre- poll war has brought out into open, all the politicians with their vulnerabilities. Since we elect a President and a Secretary every year, our building is perennially in the pre-poll mode. Any issue sparks off a display of a panoramic range of human emotions and perceptions and fragile egos. A small society with just 30 flats is in every way a miniature of what the nation is. With representations from Kashmir to Kanya Kumari, one can see all dynamics of human interaction with considerations of caste, religion, region, beliefs, values, etc. Some are tenants and some owners; a status that is rubbed in at every issue of contention as an excuse to use the casting vote. Every year a chairman and secretary are appointed more by rotation than consensus. Besides the expected- my tenure saw more progress than yours- there is a unique display of human egos and insecurities at surfaces at the slightest hint of a provocation. To think that a humble and very less preferred vegetable like the pumpkin can become an issue of contention, might sound like a hyperbole; but that was exactly what was played out recently in our society culminating in cutting of the pumpkin after prayers and distributing it like a blessing to all the residents; owners and tenants alike.

The pumpkin seed which was planted by the watchman with a green thumb grew like Jack's bean stalk, climbing all over the room of the watchman and yielding a flower right on the roof. The watchman, a displaced farmer from his soil, tended to the plant till the flower yielded a little fruit. In time this fruit grew into a large luscious pumpkin, weighing almost 16 Kg. An ideal chariot for Cinderella, isn't it? But the humble likeness of Cinderella, the watchman was ignored completely as the drama to claim the pumpkin started.

The first contention was the origin of the seed. While one resident claimed that they were the seed providers, the other claimed that the seed given by the original claimant was all dried and shrivelled and that it was the other resident who provided the magic seed. There were some who felt that the building premises belong to all the residents so any fruit on the common premises need to be shared with all.

In all this, it was completely forgotten that no resident volunteered to look after the plant. Nobody watered it or turned the soil to nurture it. There were some enthusiastic residents initially who planted some vegetables in the common area. These plants were uprooted with vengeance as the erstwhile secretary had a fancy for plants yielding seasonal flowers besides and more important; the real issue of proving a point to the old office holders. In the bargain, the garden in the building stands overgrown with weeds and the plants look completely sad and uncared for. But, this lucky pumpkin, camouflaged under the leaves, on the asbestos roof of the humble watchman grew stronger and stronger completely unnoticed by the petty considerations of the residents. However the pumpkin could not escape too long, before it could get the glory of being Cinderella's chariot, it was pulled down, sliced into pieces and sent off to the residents who had not even contributed in their thoughts to the growth of the pumpkin.

The watchman who had watched it grow like a proud father was given the chore of distributing it to all. I don't know if the watchman got a share of the pumpkin, but I know for sure that some people in the building will sleep in peace. After all, the pumpkin has not been usurped by the watchman or some other conniving office bearers. Now that the Pumpkin of contention has been eliminated, everybody can now heave a sigh of relief till the next victim is discovered and nurtured.

Thank God For The Swan Song, Sachin

After week of an overdose of a completely media created and managed hysteria, I hope everybody calls it a day and gives the likes of me a much needed break from SACHIN TENDULKAR.

He is a good cricketer. In years he has lived up to his name of being a "master blaster". But, does it warrant this kind of hero worship? From what I have read and I hope my readers correct me, he has lived, breathed and eaten cricket. His contribution to the game or existence begins and ends with just that. He loved and lived to play cricket. Besides this, I don't see anything in him that would have set him apart from ordinary and common place. In fact he did little to further the game which gave him so much of adulation. He played with passion, working with steadfast dedication BUT only for himself. When you are a part of a team sport, your team over rides your ambition. You score runs no doubt but within the span of your winning team. Ex Pakistan Skipper Imran Khan has very rightly said, "Records must be broken within the team winning. You should not be playing to break records. Records should be part of the win"

31

The only time when I, met him, I was stunned to see that a man who generates so much euphoria does not even have the courtesy to look into the camera while posing for a picture with his breathless star struck fans. Even before, he has come across to me a person who played more for himself than team India. No doubt he was a disaster as a captain of the Indian team. Today when people talk about him as a great human being, I would really like to know one instance where he has compromised his interest for humanity or even to further the game of cricket. He has been out of form for a while and besides some spurts of purely lucky and co-incidental good play, he should have hung up his boots long back and spent his huge wealth earned from the game to set up and support cricketing talent at least in his home state of Maharashtra.

I don't doubt his game or its quality. But, this is really taking it a little too far. I know we are a nation starved for super heroes and that we are obsessed with cricket. But, I never though these "handicaps' can assume such ridiculous proportions. SACHIN's speech in which he thanked his father, mother, brothers, wife, children, and even in-laws was considered as a symbol of humility! I read the transcript of the speech and watched it again and again only to spot one such word or expression of supreme humility. So, why are we making so much of ado about a guy who came played a game, played with the single minded dedication to better his game, not necessarily the team?

As far as being conferred with Bharat Ratna goes, well that is one "Barbie Doll" that is given to all the good boys and girls who have been in the good books of the dynasty party. Why else was Sardar Patel given a Bharat Ratna as an after- thought along with Rajiv Gandhi? Maybe the desperate dynasty thought that by giving a Bharat Ratna to Sachin, they can win the votes of many first time voters who worship Sachin as God and have never heard about great sports men like Major Dhyan Chand who won India Olympic Gold Medal thrice but is yet to be even considered for Bharat Ratna!

The Great Indian Tamasha

Come elections, the war drums start rolling, the battle lines are drawn clearly, the war colours are unfurled and the stage is ready for the GREAT INDIAN TAMASHA.

There isn't a moment of boredom as each party tries to undo another. So exciting is this Tamasha that for the voters for whose benefit the play acting happens is promised of a every penny worth entertainment. Well the preparations have started rather early this year due to the phenomenal Modi effect. So, till 2014 elections, all Indians must cancel their holiday plans and sit back to enjoy this Nautanki. All the Bollywood big wigs, BEWARE - Postpone all your releases as none of you can even dream of competing with the real stars of Indian politics. So, all the Salmans, Ranbirs, Shahrukhs, Deepikas, etc – take a chill pill!

To begin with the name calling....Pappu, bhondu, Fenku......I am sure even the Kindergarten kids do better than that! Then we have the usual faces of party representatives, darlings of the television, perennially in a "foot in the mouth" situation. After a whole variety of parties with an agitated TV anchor almost jumping out of the TV screen, supported by the colourful escapades of a septuagenarian spiritual guru, now in complete collusion with the TV anchor, have forgotten it all. Then there was this debate over the nuclear bill, where, while all parties screamed and shouted, this venerable scientist sat back, arms interlocked behind his head swinging sideways with utter irreverence to all the political big wigs. When he was asked a question, he was blunt enough to ask if any of the people present on panel has the capacity to set up a nuclear plant. There was this statistical data of a study conducted in some obscure group where the first time lady voters showed a preference for the "dimpled prince" thereby rubbishing some popular advertisements that have been warning politicians not to ignore the votes of women and another not at all young star who went on to heave, sigh and wish the "most eligible man" a very suggestive, husky, accented birthday wish.

A certain kurta sported by a leader has become an international brand and a certain mobile with a party branding is in available at some on line shopping portals. Wars have assumed a new definition with social media in the reckoning. As if wars on twitter and facebook were not enough, the studios have become a new battlefield where the news anchors have decided to become the voice and conscience of the nation.

Such is the power of this stage of power that anything and everything can be sacrificed and it is fair. Riots are being manufactured and once again selective appeasement is there for all to see. With the rupee hitting an all-time low and the inflation at an all-time high, the home minister has announced some austerity drives. Using a bicycle to go to work..... but where are the roads?; travelling in public transport (buses) which is the best proof for Darwin's theory of survival of the fittest. And to expect these leaders to lead by example is like a dream that Indians have stopped dreaming since independence.

Classified documents are released surreptitiously to newspapers while denials are labeled as treason. The home minister and the concerned chief ministers are suddenly pretending total ignorance of all the under hand dealings that actually has helped keeping them at the helm of affairs. All parties have their arsenal full of scoops to score in their game of one-upmanship. As the days progress one can be promised of more and more high drama.

So, the soap opera continues. One cannot even imagine in their wildest of dreams what twists and turns this great Indian Tamasha will take. The saddest part is that all this drama like a soap or a Bollywood multi starrer will NEVER have the camera zooming in on a happy - THE END.

Why Do Men Rape?

A routine day to work with the routine never ending line of traffic; but one difference -this traffic pile up was caused by curious on lookers and a posse of policemen. "Rape and murder" The words stung like tight slap. An up market locality, a road I take with my colleagues to grab a quick cup of coffee...a rape and murder there? Among all those posh residences slowly giving way to commercial space, there was this solitary empty plot, overgrown with weeds, a convenient garbage dump. It was here that the body was discovered. The shock and horror was such I did not even want to know any details of the victim or the scene of crime, just a numbing terror and horror of the cruellest of crimes- RAPE.

What makes men rapists? I cannot even use the word "beasts" as animals DO NOT rape. Rape is unique to humans and according to me it is the ultimate expression of frustration, anger and hate. The Darwinian compulsion for survival put man (read physical strength) at a position of advantage and the compulsion lasted long enough to become coded into our genes. So much so that even among those who have moved up the Maslow's pyramid, the insecurities lurk and they manifest in different ways. Man does not lose any opportunity to assert his stake on being superior even in matriarchal societies. It needn't always be expressed in violence, snide remarks, sarcastic rejoinders, temper tantrums and sometimes even sulking, brooding or wallowing in self-pity are just some ways in which man seeks attention and asserts that he is the boss. On a lighter vein, I am sure this mind-set can be ratified by any woman who drives and dares to overtake or come abreast with a male driver.

Evolution gave an upper hand to survival and consequently physical strength. Once survival is assured, what define all endeavours of a human is his needs going from the basic – physiological to the sublime- self-actualization. In a society that is dominated with a struggle for physiological needs, it doesn't take time for anybody to go back to pre-historic instincts when all actions that led to survival and satisfying basic existential needs was justified.

Any society's sanity rests on people adhering to societal rules and norms that bring about mutual respect and tolerance. But, in a society that has been split wide by blatant and vulgar disparity and a society that is still grappling with sexual stereotypes, all semblance of sanity is on a tinderbox waiting to blow up at the slightest provocation. Such is the latent anger and violence that frustration, anger and hatred that manifests in the most unthinkable forms of cruelty.

The veneer of confidence, affluence and perceived contentment of a few, causes so much of helpless anger that it lurches at the first available opportunity towards some kind of a dubious levelling. Today society is fundamentally insecure with people living in fear. There is perception of mutual threat, each of us threatened by another who could use anything in their power to be left needy. Since a large part of the population at basic, physiological needs level there is a kind of build-up in helpless anger leading to thefts, murders, riots, and yes, rapes; the ultimate expression of anger and frustration. In all these cases the victim is symbolic of a society that is a perpetrator of inequality and disparity hence the intensity of violence. Often the victims are not responsible for the perceived sense of injustice experienced by the perpetrators but they become helpless victims of their frustration.

The new manifestations of intolerance and violence is an expression of a society trying to come to terms with male stereotypes still struggling to come to terms with the fact that role as the protector is over and has to give way to that of a "partner" and a policy of the government which ensures dignity and equal opportunity to all citizens instead of sops like reservations and a cheap meal ticket. Till that happens, let no one rest in peace as each of us are potential victims of a confused chauvinistic society grappling with sexual stereotypes and unfair, inhuman disparity.

A Cocoon Called Memories

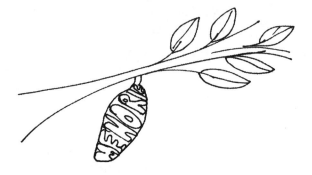

Can memories preserve the bond of blood or blood induced relations? Considering that there are so many in my clan that I have never met, never heard about, let alone speak to! Yet when I meet them all at a wedding of a niece I have never met before; there was an unmistakable and perceptible bond. Meeting my father's sisters after so many years suddenly brought memories of my father, a late cousin and it was like both of them were meeting everybody with me. There was a certain proud authority with which I staked my emotional claim over all them. In any other relationship, I would have been shrugged off or even ticked off as an aberration but here there was an indulgent acceptance. A tacit, unwritten acknowledgement- we are ONE.

Do Memories have colour, an aroma, a sound and a taste....?

I remember seeing the picture of a pond in my ancestral home and the mere sight brought the feel, the texture of fresh green water, coconut trees, red sponge like stones- particularly a stone at the edge of the pond from where we all jumped into the pond. It brought images of dark clouds almost touching the trees and the white spray of the rain through the wooden bars of the windows. The dark hill jam packed with trees and the reflection of my face in the well which seemed to dissolve out to the sides with a mere drop of a pebble.

One look at the picture of that pond and I could hear a loud splash followed by squeals of laughter and shouts. I could almost hear my aunts scolding us for making the pond all muddy and murky. I could hear the make shift water fall at the joints of the roof where we played out adventure scenes out of movies. The sound of the official rooster welcoming the sun and celebrating one more day of life, survival as we were one chicken greedy gang. The hen's disapproving and aggressive cluck as we moved her away to steal the eggs. The bleat of the goat and the moo of the cow tempting us to feed them pepper leaves and green plants which by order was not to be touched. Above all, the sound of a ripe mango falling on the ground, from branches beyond our reach and the mad greedy scramble of feet to get to the mango first.

Memories also live in smells. Fresh non chlorinated green water, wet earth, smoky kitchen full of burning embers of coconut shells, husk and stems, the warm mushy comfort of grandma's embrace, the tempered hair oil used by my aunts, ripe jackfruit, mangoes and kanji (rice gruel) on the boil.

With all my senses tingling, can taste be far behind? The taste of fresh water, the freshness of using umikari (the best tooth powder ever created) the coconut stem tongue cleaners, food eaten in a smoky kitchen, the tanginess of a make shift chutney made in an instant on the huge immovable grinding stone, rice on the boil, jackfruit leaf's spoon, rock salt, roasted cashew, watery cow's milk curd, goat's milk tea........

Oh to be home again!

Poila Boisakh VS Vishu

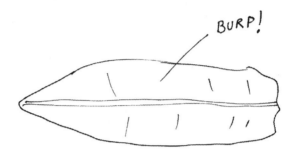

As a Keralite from Malabar, Vishu holds a very special place in my life. Arranging the "vishu kani" and seeing guruvayoorappan as vishu kani is the dream of every Malabari Mallu. Since destiny has got a "Baangal" into my life, this year, I thought that vishu celebration will be reined to a vishu kani and the sadya that follows will be Baangal in flavor. Little did I realize what a hornet's nest I had stirred!!!!

In years I have realized that just as there are there many common things that bind a Mallu and a Bong, there are many fundamental differences too. For a Mallu, food is a chore, occasionally a celebration but for a Bong it is existence! The intricacies a Bong can go into while cooking an otherwise mundane food is amazing and maddeningly granular. For a Bong life lives in these details.

Fish a binding factor, next to left leanings is the place where the essential difference sets in. A Mallu puts all the fish and the stuff needed for the gravy into one pot and simmer it till cooked. The gravy could vary but the process is much the same. But the fish specialty i.e. Mustard fish sorry "feesh" which is like the National dish of a Bong, especially a Baangal is one dish over which every Bong worth is salt makes a HUGE fuss. A true Baangal looks at mixers and grinders with a lot of skepticism. If they had their way, some inventions would have been banned by the Dhaka Convention or an equivalent body. So, the mustard for the fish has to be ground on a stone with all the anger and impatience of a Baangal house wife. The amount of turmeric and green chillies have to be measured on a chemical scale as things as fickle as instinct in the measurements can never be trusted. The way the fish is cooked, the duration, the consistency of the gravy, etc. can put even the most celebrated chefs to test.

A Bong is equally fussy about his "Begetable. Mallus eat most of their vegetables tossed in some grated coconut with just a spoonful of oil to splutter the mustard seeds. The vegetable retains its original flavor with very little almost no spices to interfere with its original taste. The veggies are usually cut into small pieces to enable an almost instant toss and stir fry cooking. But a Bong needs his veggies to go through a lot of elaborate processes; in which the vegetable apologizes for its existence. The cooking process for a vegetable makes it go through a couple of cycles of rebirth after which the vegetable is transformed beyond recognition.

A Baangal instinctively bonds with local vegetable vendor and a butcher. A Baangal's feast is incomplete without "Maangsho" which the lesser mortals call "Mutton". Since a Baangal recognizes the impossibility of butchering a just grazing goat and plucking out onions, garlic and ginger fresh from the field, the Bhegetable Bhendor and the local butcher comes to rescue. Every Baangal is genetically coded with the aroma of mustard oil. So, the oil has to be brought to a certain boiling point then the rest of the ingredients follow in regimented order. While this sacred ritual is on, only the pagan non Baangal like yours truly will suggest something as blasphemous as garlic ginger paste from any respectable FMCG chain.

However, there is a saving grace to all this fuss. The way a Baangal enjoys his food, nobody else does. A Mallu, who throws in all the food served into a mound of rice making it a mishy- mashy paste, gulping it all in one go. A Mallu won't think twice about mixing rice with fish, mutton and curd and pickle and eat it all together. For a Baangal, this kind of eating is the ultimate insult to food and humiliation of the person who has cooked it all. A Baangal will eat his food with ritualistic ardour. There is a series of servings of rice. Round one is a mouthful of rice with bitters to clear the palate, followed by a fresh serving of rice with some dal, a fried and a wet vegetable. Round three is again a fresh serving of rice and fish - jhol or shorshe, and fried fish. The concluding I round is with mutton followed by mishti doi and rosogulla, or any other sweet along with a banana thrown in. All flavours are savoured individually and a well cooked meal is unfailingly rewarded with a leaf licked clean of any traces of food and a loud satisfied BURP.

On Being Taken For Granted........

It was Valentine's Day yesterday. The hype caused by the media paid suitably by the chocolate, cards and gifts industry was evident everywhere. And I was no exception..........

So, it was heart-warming to call people who were special for you at some point in your life and wish them on the special day. To me, no other celebration can be more relevant than Valentine's Day. With so much of hatred, violence and disillusionment, what can be better than a few words of love that tends to uplift your mood and drive away the blues. Like one of my friends on being wished, said, "It's nice to know that you are still relevant"

With all these inducements working on "love is in the air" syndrome; it was but natural that I got piqued when the ONE who should have called gave it a rather cool Passover. It took some very pronounced, obvious and in-the-face hints to drive home that this is a very special occasion and hey... I am still the special one!!!

What I heard in reply to my complaint of being passed over was "of course I take you for granted. I have taken you for granted always". I retorted "WHAT!!!!!! You take me for granted!!!!" But then it set me thinking........ To begin with, I was surprised that I was not angry, in fact I found a certain warmth in that assumption. It also set me thinking........is it wrong to be taken for granted?

With some introspection, I realized that people that I have taken for granted were the ones who gave me complete emotional security. I might have been unfair to them at times but those people whose love I expected as a right were the ones who gave me the room to grow. The fact that I could take them for granted, that they were always there for me, helped me take chances in life and walk the road less taken. Even when they were removed from me, their memories were so powerful that they continued to spread their warmth in coldest of moments. Their physical presence became irrelevant but what they helped build in me became an anchor for life; an incomparable armour from all vagaries of life. In fact the memories that I have spent with them touches me at the most unexpected moments, uplifting my spirits downtrodden by hum drum of rat race.

I suppose the danger of being taken for granted is when love and trust is exploited or misused. Nor does it mean that people who are taken for granted must permit themselves to be exploited. In any exploitation the perpetrator and receiver are to blame in the same measure. But, consider the comfort of having someone who can be taken for granted. When you take a relationship for granted, it could also mean that you trust the relationship completely. Imagine if such trust could be built by parents and teachers and if children had the comfort of taking these people for granted, what a safe and secure society we would have lived in. After all, isn't all violence a fall out of our insecurities?

The Bliss Of Bitching

It is said that people of the lowest emotional and mental state talk about people. Having read such lofty ideals at a relatively young age, I shunned any such sort of object that could have led me to gossip or even discussing people. Looking back on those days, I must admit that I gained a lot of knowledge but I was such a buttonhole bore! My peers considered me well read, intelligent and were rather in awe of me but they shunned the very shadow of me.

Mercifully, the joys of bitching soon caught up with me. It did not take me very long to realize the therapeutic effect of discussing and running down people. The bond and camaraderie of sharing and analysing people is an experience that cannot be matched with any other form of entertainment.

During student days it used to be either our teachers or that special breed known as teachers' pets. Even now, when I meet my class mates we never tire of repeatedly recalling the ways in which our teachers behaved and how successful we were in getting their goat. The innocent variety of teachers was the most preferred butt of all our jokes. Then, there was this very "oh so self-assured" class mate of mine who attributed her light coloured eyes to the fact that she was born in USA. We would praise her to the skies and tell her how stunningly beautiful she is. It did not take her long to realize the intent behind the shower of praises. So, she walked up to this "apology of a teacher" whose realm of control was limited to his trousers, and complained that we all call her very beautiful. Well, the helplessness of the dramatis personae can be imagined! Similarly we had a teacher who mistakenly thought he was a dude gifted with music and humour. We, diligently fanned his ego while he, egged on by us gave quite a complex to Cacofonix. More than three decades later, we still recall these moments and relive every moment of slander that we had so sincerely indulged in.

At work, superiors and some sample co-workers provided enough fodder for entertainment during breaks and some of them even warranted messages and calls over weekends. There was this Boss who suddenly discovered a spiritual bone and went so overboard that his discourses that he would drone us all to sleep. Then there was this senior who lived in eternal terror of his seniors. He would evoke our awe by narrating experiences of Indian and foreign leaders as his own and we would always request an encore wiping our eyes streaming with emotion (laughter). Here too we had the "suck up" variety. There was one who had a memory with a very efficient updating capability. So well informed was this colleague that we christened her as "Aaj Tak" but we realized that the information provided by this colleague was quicker and juicier so we rechristened her as "Abhi Tak". My experience says that seniority always has the prospect of many a skeleton tucked away. These skeletons have a tendency to tumble out at regular intervals adding speed to gossip mills.

As long as human beings exist, their desire to control, crave respect and recognition will also be there. The smart ones do not command it but then most demand it. And as long as these people are there, bitching will continue unabated. Bitching is the best stress buster. I have heard that in some countries they have punching bags with the images of the Boss or a dart boards with the Boss's caricature. In India, where the Boss thinks he is only next to God, slander and gossip is the only respite from the drudgery of chores imposed day after day on you. So, let us continue to bitch, gossip and slander and feel the rush of all positive chemicals filling our body and mind with a warm, devilish, gleeful glow.

Of Railroads And Experiences

Train journeys were something I looked forward to as a child. I would wait anxiously for the announcement of travel concession vouchers which always signaled a train journey. The travel used to take quite a few days... like a mini holiday before the real one. The journey was a household in motion. Meticulous planning went into the food, the snacks and yes the 'surahi' from which water tastes the tastiest. The hold-all lived every bit to its name and more acting as a mini sofa in the train. I remember people even putting up cloth cradles in the train. Most train journeys saw bonding among people. While children bonded over comics and other toys, the grown -ups bonded over card games, chilled beer, and sometimes a game of chess. Travelling from Delhi to Kerala; involved a break- journey at Madras, now Chennai. Here too the great Indian family with its multiple tentacles ensured a relative whom we would have to visit before leaving for Kerala. At that time, I was sure that I had relatives in every corner of this world.

The train had taught me about the geographic and cultural diversity of India. The "chay, chay chay" in the north would become "chaya, chaya, chaya" one fine morning. The barren date palm dotted plains of Tamil

Nadu would become lush green jungles of Kerala. Today train journeys are looked down upon. People don't have the time to spend so many hours let alone days to spend on travel. I believe this has affected the quality of train journeys and the services in the train too. A couple of times when I have travelled by train recently have shown a much neglected state of trains. Most trains are infested with rodents and cockroaches. The linen provided to travellers is stale and most of the time not washed. People too have become withdrawn; all attention concentrated on when the journey will end. I feel a train journey becomes memorable if the quality of time you spend in it is enjoyable and for that, company with whom you travel is very critical. My recent train journey exposed me to a whole new experience or company.

This gentleman started with an intermittent crib about the facilities in railways. He seems to be a much more travelled person than me having crisscrossed the country several times. When he did not get much support from me, the crib turned to a humorous but sarcastic banter. As we decided to turn in, I shut my eyes, looking forward to a well -deserved sleep after a long day. Alas! that was not to be. No sooner had this gentleman touched his head on the pillow, he fell asleep....and sadly so. He snored-rather trumpeted. Soon the trumpets changed to a hardrock concert that was insisting on singing off tune. The problem was its complete lack of predictability. Had there been a rhythm to the snoring, perhaps it could have lulled the co-passengers to sleep. There would be silence for a while and then a series of groans and mumbles followed by a trumpet. To make matters worse, this person slept long and was absolutely not concerned about the inconvenience he was causing to the co-passengers. I have travelled with children, who bawl and destroy your sleep, something they can't control. But, here is a man, acutely and vociferously aware of aware of but is nonchalant about the torture he puts people through.

Poor Saddam Hussein he died without knowing about the existence of such a potent biological weapon! Besides many other things that railways need to improve, can they create a check –list to choose co-passengers too?

Mario's Goa

Sea always casts a spell. Four years in Madh Island, with an exclusive beach to myself, I have spent some of my best years watching the sea in different moods in different seasons. So, when I planned a trip to Goa, I was waiting to see the Goa that has been sold to me by Bollywood and of course Mario's sketches. So, living in an upmarket resort with a portion of Fort Aguada as its property and an exclusive beach; Goa should have been heaven but I was disappointed. Littered beaches, garbage dumps, scantily clad stoned firangs, back pack hippies....is this the Goa that people go so gaga about? To make matters worse I chose to return touching the legendary Jog falls which due to the dry spell was nothing more than a sad trickle flowing into a gorge. I was so put off that I cut short my visit and decided that if I ever felt like being by the beach, it would be Kerala.

But a few weeks back, I chanced to be a part of a wedding that was being held in Goa; South Goa. The journey took us through the reserve forests of Western Ghats and as we reached Goa, it began to rain. As we drove through the rain washed roads, I saw Mario's Goa. Idyllic, laid back with a distinct, quaint charm. As I checked into a boutique hotel this time, I saw the swimming pool stretching into green fields dotted with palms. The sea was a 10 min walk; winding though typical Goan village and Goan homes. The beach stretched out in front of us, spotlessly clean. Not a step to disturb the undulating slopes of sand. The dark clouds bent low and the sea arching up to meet it. Ah! This is heaven indeed! The day we reached Goa, it was **San Jao**, the rain festival in Goa. There were groups of merry people, young and old, wearing a wreath of flowers on their heads, singing and dancing to welcome the rains; high on *feni*; but in higher spirits; music and trumpets, dancing in the rain, diving into every pond, welcoming the rains. A popular eatery nearby; **Martins,** served crabs and other exotic sea food in Reichado sauce. What was outstanding about this eatery was its festive look, the people serving you wore bright floral shirts, the table covers were flashy and even the apron they gave to save your clothes from crab juices too were bright and cheerful. This lunch was accompanied by a Goan gentleman who moved among the tables with his Spanish guitar crooning songs of your choice and others; all this while the rain poured making the red earth in Goa brighter and more cheerful.

On asking for the way to Vasco, from a lady at a bus stop, I was pleasantly surprised to see her climb into the car and then guide us till a point from where she needed to take a diversion. Her easy trust and willingness to help was such a pleasant contrast to our city corrupted suspicion. What makes Goa so special is the atmosphere there; geographically, economically and socially. There is a general air of contentment and peace. In most cities one abhors drunken behaviour more due to the nuisance created by people who use alcohol as a ruse. But in Goa, drinking and getting drunk is also a celebration. Such is the contagion of spirit of Goa that people from most conventional roots shed all their inhibitions; and are seen lounging around in clothes they dare not wear elsewhere. People drink dance and **susegat** - chill out. Between this siesta and fiesta they just about do some work. They are happy that they live in paradise. Yes, the serpent lurks in form of real estate and drugs but it is yet to touch the spirit of Goa; at least not yet.

As we drove out of Goa, in the persistent drizzle, early in the morning, we could see churches with brightly lit altars. People were engrossed in prayers getting ready as another day rolled out for them in paradise. And we with a heavy heart headed to the battlefield where we will resume our battle with traffic, deadlines and................ a life slipping away.

Celebrity Mom

When I started writing my blog, I called it "you cannot choose your teachers" as I believe that life is a teacher. Good or bad is not our choice. A teacher from whom there is no escape; a learning that can make you or mar you forever. Such is life the teacher; it springs surprises, sometimes pleasant and sometimes painful. The onus entirely on what you make of these events and how you learn from them.

An early marriage made you an unwitting part of my learning process. As I went about riding the highs and lows of life; you too shared the bruises and the bouquets that was given to me by our TEACHERS.......... In fact for you it was tougher ....as you were so small....so vulnerable. I recall the long hours I would spend with you on the beach, building castles on the sand...seeing it getting washed way and then rebuilding it. Both of us in many ways grew up together as we shared experiences, TEACHERS that changed our lives forever.

Music was always a part of our growing up. We woke up to music, slept to music. That was the only entertainment I could give you. As a child when I used to sing with my brother, I used to feel that we should create a brother- sister group like the 'Carpenters'. That dream got lost in the business of life.

But to see you live your dream and passion makes me as proud if not prouder. And today, I am a celebrity. You have created a niche for yourself; composing and singing your own songs; way out of my influence. Your interview on TV and the huge fan following that you have today makes me feel like a celebrity. When I see your pictures, as you pluck the strings of your guitar, head thrown back in sheer ecstasy of your notes, I cannot help but feel the warm spread of pride flushing my cheeks as I with a lot of effort try to sound as matter–of-fact and say "oh he....? That's my son" and then very dismissively "ya ...he just about sings" And then say quick prayer in my mind to save you from all the "evil eyes". Now I have even begun to practice to throw tantrums like a star's mother

Looking back, I dare say our teachers have done a great job particularly on you. Your sensitivity to human feelings and your positive openness to learning have made you what you are today. Even here you have overtaken me as each scar given by life has made you stronger.......Now I am learning from you. I am proud that you have learnt more and that you have learnt better......better enough to teach me now. You are my teacher today who teaches and pampers; with the proud status of being a celebrity MOM.

I Am No Super Woman

With the Women's' Day just around the corner, I recall the recent furore caused by the comment of a judge about women's empowerment causing problems in the family and social structure. His comment had a lot of women activists crying hell and fire. But, come to think of it, has this empowerment made the lot of women any better? Let us not look at their status vis-à-vis their position in society in comparison with the men. My question is purely about the state of women today.

To begin with one needs to decide if empowerment needs to happen at the mental, social or economic level.

Destiny made me a part of a matriarchal family system, there I observed that empowerment was the thing of the mind. Socially, a male child was preferred even there and was welcomed with much fanfare. There was clear behavior tenet laid out for the male and female child. Yet, when the situation demanded, the women in the family within those constraints took complete charge. My paternal grandmother married to a handsome but unworldly wise man had to be cold, practical and decisive to protect her family's interests. My mother's eldest sister had to take on the reins of the family to protect the wealth from being squandered away by her wayward brother, my uncle. While these women took charge, there were other women in the family who were very happy and content being a mother or a wife. Neither of them to me looked oppressed or unhappy. They were all empowered and emotionally secure. Never did I hear about physical abuse or mental abuse even if extramarital alliances happened on a routine basis. In fact the legal wife was magnanimous enough to accept the other woman as sister who she rightly felt was as much a victim as she is. So, I was not shocked or surprised when in a recent family gathering my mother with all due respect, introduced me to my father's "elder brother" born of a different woman/ grandma.

In north India too, I observed not just well defined gender roles but a certain cruelty and insecurity attached to it. My friends had unhappy grandmothers and mothers. Living under the same roof, there seemed to be a power struggle of sorts where the power was manifested in the control of the male attention. With so much of suspicion and insecurity, violence is a natural fall out. The male child was a long term investment made by the parents for their old age. So, the girl who would share the fruits of investment was expected to contribute as a return of investment, hence the dowry. The history of the world is testimony to the fact that economic considerations have always led to struggle for power and control and then the fall out of the struggle- oppressor and the oppressed.

The only difference in the two regions was the way it was administered. One did it with outmost subtlety and the other was terribly in the face.

Today these dividing lines have thinned and I feel a woman has become completely a victim of economic considerations. Today a woman is expected to be a super woman. Her ability to become an earning family member improves her marriageability. Once married she is expected to take on or share the economic burden of the family and be a dutiful wife or mother at the same time. This super woman is every bit like the deity with multiple hands, multitasking almost with mechanical precision. Like a well programmed robot she switches roles with both functional and emotional alacrity. Today you will see expressions of pity on people's faces when you tell people that you are a homemaker!

I think somewhere along the way in which the women's empowerment is headed, needs a paradigm shift. The empowerment has to begin in the mind. I don't think any empowerment will take place by women denying their strengths as women, by competing with men to be their equal or even better them and the most dangerous – perpetuating a new kind of chauvinism.

A man who does not respect a woman will not respect her notwithstanding her economic or social status.

Does the woman then want his submission through coercion?

Does the woman want such a character's respect?

Will any thing; force or friendship; change him?

Will she recognize that what she is trying to tame is flawed by nature and threat will only suppress the instinct?

Why does she need a man? Does she need him for companionship? Does she want him for her security?

Or, the most important, does she need a man at all?

The day a woman is able to answer these questions, prioritize these considerations; she will be liberated and in every sense happy, content and empowered.

To Live To Love..........

How does one cope with the loss of one's shadow, a friend, and a soul mate? Hopefully he is in happy hunting grounds. But....is he be happy there? Won't he miss me .....like I miss him?

Born to Juliet a blue blooded German Shepherd and a wayward Labrador..... they were an ideal blend of the best of qualities of both the breeds. Sonic, a raggy shaggy fur ball, walked up to me, sniffed my feet, curled up and slept; accepting me as his mom. Soni, his chubby golden sibling, slept blissfully, content in herself. Sonic was chosen to be adopted but the pretty Soni tempted us into taking her too. As, I carried the two fur balls to my home, little did I know, that they would become not just a part of our life, but also our identity.

Soni, the pretty girl was the very symbol of dignity. She had German Shepherd like features and the golden coat of a Labrador. Her coat was shiny and clean, her pink nose a little snooty but very pretty. She was mature and intelligent and sort of looked down upon Sonic's playful juvenile behaviour. She loved going for walks, swimming and drives. She looked forward to being given a bath and would then spend hours preening over her glossy coat. With such good looks can arrogance be behind? She littered only once as a result of an accidental mating with Sonic. After that she never mated leaving per poor mate Sonic completely high and dry. We lost her in 2009 when she did not survive a surgery to remove her uterus.

Sonic....... The coat and body of a German Shepherd but the face of a Labrador was wrongly named as he hated music. He was a tramp. His rough coat never shone in spite of all the grooming. He hated baths and wanted to be scratched perennially. He was very talkative, exuberant and very demanding. His keen nose could smell food and his sixth sense helped him smell food kept just about anywhere at home. A terror and night mare of all dogs and people in the vicinity, he was petrified of Soni. Like all self-respecting men, he never took any chances with her and was completely in awe of her. When she would come on heat, high drama would unfold at home. He would whine and plead and she just looked away in complete deaf nonchalance. When his appeals to Soni went in vain he would plead to us to intervene. He was very expressive and gave us a very vocal piece of his mind whenever we went out of town. After Soni left us, it was Sonic who took it upon him to make sure that we don't miss her much. He became more of my "Sonny dog" loving me for just being there....loving me with no expectations ....unconditionally.

Together they meant security both physical and emotional. After 14 years I am now relearning to lock the door. I am painfully aware of the absence of the patter of feet following me, the swish of a tail that upset my cutlery and the jar of biscuits, a favorite bribe for our long working hours. Had it not been for them I would not have survived some of the darkest moments of my life.

Life without Soni was sad....but life without Sonic is painful. He rests under a chikoo tree in Whispering Meadows......but somehow he lives on.......

MIL- The Brand New Status

With this new found status, I ought to feel all hoity-toity. There should be a certain swish and arrogance in the way I walk after all I am a mother- in-law of a "soni kudi" both literally and metaphorically due to her Punjabi origins. Like my friends advise me, I should start wearing trail blazing sarees with complicated designer bindis and when I call out to my DIL..... well even the nature should stand in suspended animation waiting for the commanding diktat of the MIL!!!!

Now....this is where the huge disconnect sets in. I have begun to have serious doubts about myself...am I really a misfit in the society?

To begin with I was warned that I have lost my son forever.....well, instead of feeling bad I am rather happy about it. I used to feel a pang of regret every time he left home as I used to wonder how he would cope with loneliness as all moments alone are not solitude. This time when my son left, I was happy that he will not have to return from work to an empty home...he will have the company that he has chosen to be with. I have always felt that the most precious claim is the claim of the heart and to recognize that my son has actually found a soul mate is indeed a very liberating and elevating feeling. It's as if I have one more person to share that emotional responsibility. Other material things have never mattered to me anyway.

I was told about how my DIL would slowly take control of my son and then my home. WOW .....I have been looking so much forward to retire from mundane chores at home so that I can spend the rest of my life writing and reading ....take long walks in the solitude of early morning Bangalore mist..... I would in fact say cheers to this fear and pray fervently that this come true. Imagine being free of the usual mundane shopping, cooking, cleaning, entertaining routine? What can be more heavenly than that?

My reaction to having a DIL is to have a friend with whom I can share some girlie moments. I can share so many things with her that I cannot share with "guys". Whether it is sharing a unique dish called "paani puri cornflakes" or if it is sharing little asides and digs on the "guy" behaviour and attitudes...I am doing things that I have never done. Surrounded by boys all the time, it's as if that girlie part in me was dead and buried. My first shopping sojourn with her was so much of fun. We actually went berserk trying anything and everything. It was so much fun when she would try something and step out for a second opinion; the girlie thrill of bitching about dress sense, hairstyles and tacky colours. It's so much fun to have a co-conspirator against the "guys" where we share a knowing laugh and leave them mad at their unimaginative wild guesses.

Well, as of now having a DIL has done wonders......it has actually awakened a girlie teenager in me!

Happy Birthday Kasab!

Happy birthday Kasab!

Hope you had a lovely day!

I hope the jail authorities gave you something interesting to eat...I understand it's difficult to eat Biryani every day!

Your simplicity is so endearing. Almost childlike...you know. You cry sometimes and then laugh with glee. You have in your special adorable ways kept the jail authorities guessing.

Your sense of fun could teach a couple of lessons to the entertainment industry as you keep leading investigators on a wild goose chase.

You are a living example of courage even in the face of extreme adversity; even when your parents disowned you and your Nation turned its back on you. You laughed in sheer courage as the charges were read out against you in court, you openly challenged the judicial system of the largest democracy in the world.

To top it all you are so unassuming...you are a theme for so many shows, the TV channels treat you as an icon that sent their TRP ratings soaring. You even managed to overshadow the so called martyrdom of super star cops. Still you sit in the protection of a Spartan cell, unaffected by all this attention and adulation.

But then yesterday was your day! On your birthday, the special gift, the three blasts in the most crowded areas of Mumbai was a tribute to your courage and dare devilry. You must have slept well yesterday, as the blasts were the ultimate icing in the cake. It happened just where you and your friends were. Did the jail authorities allow you to watch the fireworks and its gory aftermath? Even your best friend the Home Minister, remarked that the fireworks were "Planned". Remember such compliments from him are rare. You would have laughed once again to see the hapless people rave and rant against the Government of India.

Your friends, some perhaps even trained you for action have sent you a loud and explosive message

HAPPY BIRTHDAY KASAB—HAVE A BLAST

The Forgotten Finishing Line

I'd rather be a forest than a tree....yes I would, if I could....... Simon and Garfunkel can really play havoc. Something in me has begun to murmur that this is not the life I bargained for. Sanitized work spaces, insulated from the vagaries of weather. People pushed into compartments called work space. Then miles and miles of metal shimmer, all headed like headless chicken to God knows where? Every face, taut and tense; waiting to explode. The saving grace; a stray glimpse of lovers; the sweet madness in their hearts creating a halo of magical oblivion.

Am I being sucked into a renunciation mode? Somehow, the desire to fight, the desire to resist and the desire to prove myself is not there anymore. I look at the milling crowds around me and am filled with a painful sense of emptiness. Something in me tells me that this is not what I want....I have gone wrong somewhere...terribly wrong....where is the sense of achievement? Or to put it honestly – what am I trying to achieve? And more pertinent...do I really want to achieve?

More than ever I want to get away to some place that has not yet been ravaged by ambition and progress. A place where people do not live in stacked compartments, one piled above the other, a place where people do not spend evenings, robot like blinking in a stupor like daze at the idiot box. A place where people do not gobble up some junky fare to fill their bellies. A place where people do not even have a right to their share of earth, sky and sun. A place, where one is controlled by the uncontrollable, transient, tyrant; Time.

In our blind race for material affluence, we have lost sight of the real finish line. In this race, unlike the fabled rabbit we have not slept off... on the contrary, we have slogged so much that the finish line has become irrelevant. After all what do we all want at the end of the day? Are we all not on the lookout for contentment? Don't we all want satisfaction? Don't we all want peace? Deep in our hearts we all seek: A place where I have all the time to gaze at the rising and setting sun. A place where I can be lulled into slumber by the cry of a koel. A place where I can sit back and read, with the sound of the rain gushing through leaves. A place where lazy, warm afternoons are spent lolling on the coolness of a plain scrubbed floor. A place where evenings carry the aroma of wet, water sprayed earth. A place where the evening lamp and smoke from the kitchen chimneys lend a perfect prelude to the star spangled night.

BMTC vs DTC

Now that I am back on the roads of namma Bengaluru....one cannot help but notice some typical traits of Bangalore Traffic. I feel this is unique to Bangalore but I am sure that all metros have something characteristic and typical of them.

To begin with I salute the BMTC buses. They not just stop at designated Bus Stops, they stop just about anywhere. All one needs to do is extend a hand and drop an intention that you could board a bus and lo and behold they stop! So, isn't it natural that the BMTC buses with such noble and strict adherence to their dharma, are bound to have a certain arrogance and swagger. Hence they call the shots on the road! They rarely give way to other selfish vehicles who do not share their exalted Dharma! Sometimes when a BMTC bus gives me the right of way, I am so shocked that I don't move. Then I am torn between the dilemma of jumping out of the car and bending low to do a 'namaskara' or should I pray to the almighty for such grace? These BMTC buses have earned strangely located bus stops too. There is always a bus stop at the end of a flyover creating a much avoidable pile up of traffic. In the same way, there are many bus stops located immediately after a red light. None of these hitches deter the nobility of the BMTC buses behaviour. They follow their Dharma. They wait patiently at the bus stop for the passengers to pile in till they spill over. No doubt BMTC has introduced special fleet of buses which is uppity in their appearance, but still the humble BMTC goes about its Dharma of being a means of transport for the common man.

Now contrast this with DTC, Delhi Transport Corporation. Wider roads, well planned traffic lights, state of the art bus stops and with the support from the Delhi Metro. The DTC buses just don't stop at the bus stops. As a Delhiite I used to gauge from the movement of the bus if it would stop before the bus stop or after. Most of the time one gets into a battle of wits with the bus driver. The bus driver without any specific training is adept at the art of gauging if the people at the bus stop will come to catch the bus before or after ...accordingly they plan their strategy. These DTC buses are great pranksters too....they slow down as if to stop and the passengers rush to board they drive off...hahahahah! What a joke! DTC buses are sticklers for orderly number of people seated in the bus, hence they dislike taking in too many passengers. I suppose they decide on a fancy what number of passengers should be seated in a bus and move accordingly. It's a Bus not a container into which people can be packed like sardines! Most DTC buses prove the Darwinian maxim of survival of the fittest!

Delhi has some private buses running too. Initially they were called red line buses as they were painted Red. Somehow, these buses took their colour rather seriously and behaved accordingly; true to their colour. Since these buses ran on the profit earned from the number of passengers, they not just stopped at bus stops; they pleaded the passengers to board their buses. Tempted them with their choice of music and let people board and get off anywhere. Such was the sense of competition, that they raced with the other buses to get to the Bus Stop sooner so as to grab more passengers. Quite often the drivers of these Red line buses were untrained so they usually decimated other vehicles that crossed their path. Such was the rush to grab passengers that the brakes were ignored and the bus would stop after it had parked itself INSIDE the bus stop! These Red Line buses earned the notoriety of being "killer" buses.

And the Delhi government with their characteristic myopia changed the colour of the buses to blue so that people would not get affected by the Red colour of the buses!

The Dilemma Of Extended Umbilical Cord

A dilemma that most Indian parents face is when to cut the emotional umbilical cord? Even a parent like me who struggles to maintain stoic objectivity in my relationship with children, stumble ....there is always the nagging thought that "no one knows better than mom" So, whether it is a warm oil massage, or rustling up a favourite dish....the motivation behind all this activity is just one factor-: I have known my child more than others, the nine month edge; hence no one think better for the child".

My experience and experiments as an Educator tells me that the extended umbilical cord often does more damage than good. This cord puts so much of emotional pressure on the child that it stifles independent thought and action. Crippling the child permanently...never letting the child really grows up. Such is the ambit of this cord that it creates a protective blanket around the child insulating the child from all trials and tribulations in life. Crippling the child permanently; never letting the child "grow up" enough to take decisions in life.

I have wondered when the wife in a woman gives in to the mother. I have seen women live away from their husband with whom they share (supposedly) a much more intimate relationship (at least technically). What triggers this sudden preference of roles? What makes a woman forget all their marriage vows to go to some remote location only to cook and feed the child; leaving the husband to fend for himself. The wife in the woman rests assured that the relationship with the husband is secure (ab is umar mein jayega kahan!) and so she chooses the other relationship which is constantly facing onslaughts of hormone driven temptations.

In this gamut of relationships what applies to Peter does not apply to Pan. For example if the husband does not snap the umbilical cord with the appearance and establishment of the wife....then the poor man has no peace. So, the problem begins when History repeats itself! The entry of an inferior creature, young, nubile, inexperienced, upstart, etc, is viewed with a lot of resentment. This is a necessary evil to ensure the occurrence of the circle of life! This one element sometimes chosen after many rejections becomes the catalyst for many more disasters in future. So, while History unfolds its set pattern, the parents are lost, disillusioned and devastated!

The parents, who have lost out on precious time with each other, are now suddenly thrown together. In this entire cycle, the loser is the woman, the wife and as a fall out the husband. In the twilight of their life they end up playing nannies to their grandchildren and bear the insults piled on them by their own flesh and blood that cannot dump their parents for the fear of loss of inheritance. And they all continue to shamelessly exist: parents at the mercy of their ungrateful, insensitive children. Children who see no use of their parents except to look after their children; Children, who never forgive their parents for not snapping the Umbilical cord!

Au Revoir

My dear teachers and my children, I have to call it a day. Why?

I cannot be deaf to the voice of my conscience and heart. I know that you will understand me as you all have been a part of me. I am guilty of walking away, of being unfair to my team and to my children who have tasted the joy of an unfettered fearless mind. My Children, you have understood the huge burden of responsibility that comes with such freedom. I hope you too live life by the ideals that I taught and displayed to you.

Last one year, in company of people committed to "ideology" I have learnt to be very wary. I never knew ideology can be cloaked in such crude, crass and mundane masks. I never knew that Ideology can be such a kill joy; such an enemy of happiness. No surprise then that I have turned to the ultimate hero of free thought and liberty – Che. No doubt the sheer honesty of his realizations juxtaposed to human vulnerability has made him a timeless hero. Hearts throb of anyone who believes and stands up for freedom. Call it mid life crisis ....I am once again hopelessly in love with "Che".

We are all such suckers for ideology. We live in a constant guilt of being better than the underprivileged brother. And this guilt sometimes overpowers you to step into the haloed circle of keepers of ideology. Like I did; a year ago when I walked into an assignment. After two years in the corporate and six years before that in Protestant regimentation, I was a sitting duck, a complete sucker for idealism.

Taken in, by the special effects of the elaborate patterns made on the forehead of a senior citizen, a querulous tone that spoke of a life full of sacrifice and the unassuming yet alert demeanour of another quiet observer, I walked into a final round of interview. Here I was confronted with more idealists who appeared then as people who merely 'existed' in other mundane roles for mere sustenance while their souls sang in unison for the glorified Bharat.

Sniff, sniff, sob, sob.......

Damn it! Was my sixth sense pissed drunk?

Such was the heady romance that I failed to see the warning signs. Their illogical rigidity on rituals for special effects, The superficiality of knowledge and information where even the very basics like difference between spirituality and religion lost all clarity. Their myopia to information; where Bhagat Singh and other revolutionaries were worshipped as heroes of the Hindu Bharat, totally ignorant to their atheist and communist leanings. The completely fake and half baked claim to knowledge of yoga, the outward portrayal was that of a one big happy family where one had to tolerate the good, the bad and the ugly. So, my team had to sit through boring nonsensical sessions of download where all including those on the podium except the speaker, slept. The idea of one big happy family was driven in through prayers and more prayers, rituals and of course cauldrons full of slurry messy bise belebath and mosuru anna. Where people washed their hands into the plate they ate out of ....I must say I was thankful that nobody tried rinsing their mouth into the plate! The one big family, ideal was always restricted to the organization. Your personal front i.e. your spouse or children were never a part of this very ideal picture of BharatMata.

Soon I realized that the people I am dealing with are clueless about Education or learning. Each armed with some fancy thought and ideas have made the organization a playground for experimenting novices. As the veneer of this craziness grows transparent, the hidden agenda behind the craziness is clear; the age old adage of "keeping employees on their toes". How sic! All this coupled with the theatrics of a senile, wily, old man who very ironically, in a Gandhian way, demands (not commands!) Public display of respect and bulldozes and blackmails with amazing illogical shamelessness; only to have his way.

Though I am guilty of leaving you all without a warning, I hope you never forget the true meaning of Education and Learning. I will cherish memories of a team that did not hesitate to walk any amount of extra miles for me. Of a group which mirrored my passion for learning; a group that proved to all sceptics that a school can be a really happy place.

Unconditional Love

Shanta elayemma (younger mother), my mom's youngest sister; a result of middle age adventure by my grand parents. She was incredibly beautiful with an innocent childlike smile. I remember her wearing a long skirt, (a pavada) and blouse. She wore red very often which made her baby pink complexion even more enviable. She would quietly walk into the kitchen and wait to be served. Any delay would make her angry and off she would go sulking and complaining about the inefficiency of the person who was in charge of kitchen that day. Her complaints were taken very seriously, when matyamma; my mother's eldest sister would give a mouthful to the person who made that grave blunder. Her bathing sessions would be long after which she would come upstairs to get "dressed". Oh how she loved being pampered! We would comb her hair; make her wear matching bindis with her dress. Much to our frustration we realized all our efforts were so useless! She was already so beautiful!

She could never read and write but loved hearing stories and we loved narrating stories to her too. Looking back on those days, it never struck me as strange that she was the only illiterate member in our family!

She loved children and children loved her. I don't ever remember a child not wanting to go to her. With us, she was a perfect play mate. She hated our boisterous games but loved dancing, singing and acting. We all would be such a rapt audience with continuous "encore!" She would fight with us if she ever lost a game and yes, Matyamma would make sure that she never lost! The winner was reprimanded with knowing stern looks and the message would sink in "you bloody well lose!"

Due to some strange phobia, she never accompanied us anywhere. She seemed so happy in the large sprawling home and its lush green surroundings. We would beg and plead and tell her how beautiful the city is. We would describe the dazzling shops, the busy streets and the buildings stacked one on top of the other. She would hear us out in sheer wonder but resisted every attempt to be taken out. She seemed to have a morbid fear for vehicles. Even when she fell ill, the doctor was called home; she never stepped out of the compound to see the doctor.

Her wishes were always our commands. Her wishes used to be something as simple as a pavada with green leaves, a purple chaand pottu, yellow glass bangles, etc. But anybody who was told about her desire would make it a point to get it.

As I grew older, I realized that Shanta elayamma was different from us; she was special. She was a case of "mongoloid syndrome" But she was a part of the family; a part of all our trials and tribulations. She was never made to feel the pain of being different. In fact she knew she was different and she was loved and pampered for it; a feeling she returned it to us in equal measure. Nobody dreamt of a need to send her away to a "home". She was adored the way she is. Hurting her was the worst blasphemy one could imagine! If anyone of us would make her cry; the repercussions were painful. Everybody at home and in the family would put in a "tut- tut" till you swore never to make that irreparable blunder again. Such was her place in our family.

None of my grandparents or my mothers' siblings or my cousins who lived with her day in and out had read books on human mind or psychology; all they knew is that she is different from others and so she needs more protection, more care, more love ....unconditional love.

A Star Is Born

Wasn't it just yesterday?

- When you would listen as if in trance lying in the cradle to Jim Reeves singing his soul out?
- When you broke into uncontrollable sobs when Annie's Song was played?
- When you broke my desire for a baby girl when you repeated my favourite lullaby as "mere ghar aayi ek "NANGI" pari?
- When you with your characteristic pronunciation were irritated when I could not figure out that you wanted me to sing "Patte patte yum num num" to be understood as "pat a cake pat a cake baker's man"
- When you would repeat Anup Jalota as "jagad mein jodi nate hai; apne apne kallon tatiye; sab hi pate ye de. Original being Jagat mein job hi aate hain, apne apne karmon ka fal, sab hi patein hai.
- When you stood on the stage, barely visible and recited "Thirsty Crow" in a musical manner with your feet tapping to the music.

- When you won the very first prize for singing Annies' song. This time no tears, no mispronunciations, only melody.
- When you sang "oh re taal mile nadi ke jal mein" and the recording was misplaced by a callous teacher.
- When you got a guitar as a birthday gift and that brat brother ruining the surprise with "Dadu we have NOT bought you a guitar"
- When you were "caught" by your Bro playing guitar in a state that would put even Narcissus to shame.
- When you discovered the sheer magical power of "Hotel California" in a Christian school.
- When you were known for "Country roads" and "seasons in the sun" and would sing it to the point of fatigue.
- When you stepped out of my influence to sing a more contemporary "Yaaron" and "Pal"
- When you practiced and represented your college in the theme song from Love Story.
- When you struggled to learn the intricacies of Simon and Garfunkel's strumming.
- When you would earn free train rides thanks to "Bheege hoonth tere"
- When you were wedded to the guitar whom you indulgently called "Ms Nair" as you and her are inseprable
- When you began to get more and more popular on U tube
- When you decided to follow your heart like always and recorded your own very first song "O mere Khuda"

Yesterday, when you performed, these memories flooded in from my heart to my eyes which were too clouded and proud to realize that "a star is born".

Memories

Memories are made of strange images, sounds and smells. They would look very commonplace to somebody really not associated to it but to the person who has lived it; they are actually the "bliss of solitude".

These flashes are usually not connected to any incident or person but they somehow linger and keep coming back to your mind.

One of the oldest memories I have is the smell of my grandma. As I would snuggle up to her and bury my face in the loose folds of her stomach, she had a mushy smell so warm and comforting.

Dec1971, Indo-Pak war, black out. My father in a warm Russian over coat, with the torch in his pocket; I would curl up to him and hear him narrate incidents during the Chinese aggression. This image also brings forth the sound of the air raid siren followed by an all clear siren. The sound of the News reader on All India Radio, announcing the bombings by Pakistan on Agra (terrifyingly close to Delhi). India at War image: The trenches, the sand bags, the training to save oneself from a bomb. Glass windows blackened, pitch dark evenings.

Then teenage took over and memories are clouded and crowded with physical sensations; trivialities like the crushes, costumes, comrades, compulsions and commitments. Nothing of this time endures, like a slice of life not lived at all! Youth being no better, the heady energy lead from one tunnel to another leading nowhere really till your life stops rocking and settles in the comfort of a soul mate. Here memories are dominated by people with an occasional break of the warm winter sun, the burst of spring colours at traffic islands, the post spring exam flavored autumn.

By virtue of matrimony, I got to travel and then begins a profusion of memories. The crispy smell of icy blue sky in Ladakh, the profusion of stars at high altitude, the chilling water of Indus, the trees all aflame in autumn.

My first visit to Mumbai, the business capital, in the first summer rains it looked like a huge shanty city. Till I saw the sea. Then on, all senses were overpowered by the aromas and moods of the sea. Then, there was a lull as I journeyed one city to another, painfully identical, memories being only of people who walked in and out of my life.

Asif by means of compensation, life brought me once again to the lap of Nature, surrounded by the Satpuras and with the Mowgli jungle just a stone's throw away, the city on the banks of Narmada was an ideal compensation for being away so long from Nature. One enduring memory I have is of driving through the jungle in heavy rain. On an impulse, I pulled up and got out to see the jungle in rain. The deep tiger jungle was ALIVE. There was a profusion of sounds of rivulets gurgling as the rains had activated all streams. The jungle itself looked like a huge sage sitting in deep meditation as the water poured down its branches and leaves. The smell and sounds of the Narmada as she rushed through the marble gorges. The feel of the dhuan dhar as the water crashed down creating a smoke like spray. Away from the city, even food has a lingering aroma and smell. The aroma and taste of the Baatis and Bharta baked in cow dung cakes with kaithe ki chutney still makes your taste buds tingle with excitement.

At dusk or evening, as I swear, curse and manoeuvre through the Bangalore tragic my mind wistfully races to the banks of Narmada and the sonorous sound of the wooden bells around the neck of the cows as they return home. Each cow, scrubbed clean with combed manicured tails look at you with suspicion and you wonder if you have even begun to smell of a city? In the mild dusty orange twilight, one sees and feels the magic of godhuli as the sun rests behind the Satpuras giving way to the moon and the stars to weave their magic.

AZADI

Azadi certainly comes at a price. Very often I have wondered, do the human species deserve Azadi? Aren't we all slaves of our upbringing, the subtle and blatant biases that are slowly released into our system right from birth? Are human beings capable of handling the cruel and harsh implications of Azadi?

I have been watching articulate young men and women from Kashmir talk of Azadi. After being used year after year as a ready tool for political propaganda, the Kashmiris have made their mind up. The young men and women on the streets of Kashmir are not terrorists. Don't conveniently blame the madrasas or the cloak and dagger games of the neighbor across the border. These young men are fed up. They have had enough of the yoyo sharing of power between the so called heirs and heiresses of Kashmir.

I cannot but recall a character in Mahaswetadevi's short story on Dopdi Here a tribal woman activist, gang raped on the orders of Senanayak the BSF officer who had captured her alive. He is proud of his prize catch and happier that he has taught her a lesson. In the morning when she is to be presented in front of the Senanayak, she refuses to cover herself, breaks the pot of water offered to her and walks proud and naked in her just and much raped status and challenges him by pushing him with her sore breast ......and for the first time Senanayak is terrified; terrified of this unarmed target.

Haven't we pushed Kashmir to this desperation? Youthful optimism is a very heady sensation and for this optimism to give way to desperation reflects how hopeless the situation is. For the Kashmiri youth to come out on the streets even at the cost of being gunned down, itself is statement of how they are driven to desperation. No doubt they are demanding unconditional Azadi. Maharaja Hari Singh is history and so is Simla Agreement. One needs to open a new chapter; start from the scratch and rebuild the lost trust of Kashmir.

Maybe this is the backdrop in which we need to view Arundhati Roy's statement. I salute her for articulating the cry of the Kashmiri youth. Like she said, both India and Kashmir have had enough of each other in this state. Both of them need to rework and recreate an equation where Kashmir can have the status of a Nation State.

It is easy to fall into the comfort of jingoistic Nationalism. Geographical boundaries should never be drawn in the minds of the people. Two world wars are a testimony to that. Keeping in mind the truth that change alone is permanent; we need to consider alterable geographical boundaries lest Nations and its people bleed to death.

The Feature I Wish My Smart Phone Had!

To begin with I must admit that mobile phones have taken away a lot of surprise from our lives..... Ah! Remember those days where the heroine is heading towards a cliff due to some misunderstanding. Think of that rising crescendo as the hero is trying to reach her after grappling with so many threats and just about makes it fraction of a second before the fatal leap to death. So many movies would not have been super -duper hits as all their success was dependent on the uncertainty caused by lack of communication. I grew up holding Indian Railways and the Post and Telegraph departments solely responsible for many crises that happen in people's life. Somehow these departments had some kind of a bonding with fate. These three would play havoc in people's lives till an angry hero or heroine threatens God with dire consequences.

And then those good old telephones with those round dials were so majestic. When it would ring, your heart would actually dance and sing "mere piya gaye Rangoon kiya hai wahan se telephone....." Can anybody forget the sheer romance of "jalte hain jiske liye......." The telephone like the telegram always created a flurry of activity. The loud imposing ring was never a disturbance ....one never thought of switching it off.....it just had to be attended to.

As a part of the generation that has actually seen both the worlds. I must say that Mobile has somehow made communication very common place. No doubt it is very convenient to have anybody and everybody a call away but then somehow the mystery element of a phone call is lost in the sands of time. A lot of young people wonder how we managed walking up to the phone and talking into a wired and stationary instrument.

Now these little terrors have become mini computers! So, there is no escape now. Your work like a hound is bound to track you wherever you go. So, your candle lit dinners have to be shared with the flash of the smart phone's screen crying for your attention. With their ability of reaching out to a lot of network and even work where network connectivity is weak, I wonder if we are slowly becoming human work horses!

But somewhere at the back of all this black and whitish nostalgia, I cannot ignore the boon of having a smart phone in hand. But yes....there are some features that need to be added to make my phone really smart! A smart phone should ideally have a sensing system that would save a lot of heartburn and embarrassment and thereby ensure overall well- being and happiness.

- Delayed relay of messages between teenagers and their parents; especially when it is monetary in nature. How about a 24 hour delay?
- The facility of a mild electric shock amounting to a slap on the cheek of a teenager when the parent touches a button.
- Sales messages to be returned to the sender in such a way that the sender's system gets jammed
- Certain calls to be denied with a suitable automated reply (especially the ones that come from the Boss at unearthly hours and unexpected places)
- E mails with dead- lines to be delayed (preferably after the dead line)

- E mails with dangerous spelling errors and communication lapses to bounce. I am sure the spell check tool to be made more sensitive
- Abusive and angry mails to be sent to the Boss but only for the satisfaction of the sender. This mail could be routed into a box called the "Punch bag Box"
- Assistance to be given by pop up support from a vibrant dictionary that supplies the phrases and words that one is fumbling for while writing a mail

Well the list is long....but for now, these features would make your phone really smart!

Parents Need Education

One thing that I can vouch for after almost 6 months in the hot seat (Principal) is that parents need education much more than children. Children are great learners and great teachers. Their unbridled curiosity keeps the teachers on their toes pushing them way beyond what the teachers presumed was their limit. In this happy blend where the taught becomes the teacher but the greatest kill joys are parents.

Somewhere along the parents have come to a realization that parents who find faults with the school, the parents who are cantankerous in meetings and the parents who have an aura of "I know it all and have been there" are the parents whose child gets most attention. In fact such parents are the greatest kill joys who in fact interfere with the learning process in a child.

One is the over-zealous variety. Most hail from supposedly families of high achievers and they want their off spring to be a shade better. Well, the ambition is noble but extremely torturous to a child. The child sees the school as the only place where he can be free from the leash of his mother's aspirations. Naturally, the child then let go and tries to live his suppressed childhood in those few hours in school.

Then we have the Parent who feels that they know it all and have no regard for the nobility of a teacher's profession. They tend to look at teachers as one of those grovelling employees just a shade above the helping hands. No doubt the kind of dole that is handed over to the teachers' warrants such conceptions but then these parents are a huge source of embarrassment for their children as they cringe in discomfort as they know what kind of an encounter the parent would possibly have with the teacher.

After these come the traditionalists. They tell you nonchalantly that we are free to hammer their child as the child only learns like that. They want all the answers to be given to the child which the child will cram with expertise. Words like imagination and creativity is the greatest anathema to such parents. Their children are wonderful samples of programmed learning where they score very well without learning anything.

The new age parents are a class in themselves. They do not have much time for their children. Such parents are very happy as long as the grades are above average and they are not hassled too much. Some of them to save the bother of teaching their children even go to an extent of doing the work assigned to them. Some of them are perhaps so caught in their world that they take instructions given to the child literally. To them children are like one of their KRA that they need to attend to.

First generation learners are the next category who take every word of the teacher as gospel truth and follow it religiously. They are definitely a great deal of comfort to the teacher but then can never become partners in learning.

And now the saddest, the criminal parents!!! These parents are completely insensitive to their children. They abuse them and cripple their young minds with insensitivity and mindless violence verbally and physically. One wonders why no laws are enacted to save children from their parents???

Nature Vs Man

When nature gives a glimpse of her power, all that we mortals can do is shudder. All we can do is to look incredulously as nature rips apart all the expertise of man. All we can do is wonder why today? Why now?

Everything was so perfect....The homas went on as per schedule; all arrangements went on like clockwork. True to the character of sangh, everybody volunteered and participated, no work too small or insignificant....The evening was good too....everybody was all dressed, proud to belong to the edifice whose lokaarpan was to be graced by none other than the Chief Minister. The evening was started by a child prodigy presenting keertans. As the song progressed, there was a sudden breeze, cool, soothing full of the scent of wet earth. The diehard optimist in me insisted that the rain will only bring us a much needed respite from heat.

But even before we blinked, the breeze assumed a furious form. It raged and raved, and the rain came crashing right through the reinforced awning. The guests moved away into the corridors in stunned silence. Such was the shock that in spite of the police urging people to move to shelter, no body rushed...everyone moved completely overawed by the fury of Nature. There was hushed silence ...some parents pulled out their cameras and clicked the devastated remains of the stage which just a few moments ago was an image of festivity. No a person complained or cribbed....in fact all seemed to recognize the helplessness of man against the power of Nature.

The program went on...a little delayed amidst utter chaos and confusion. The chief guest arrived too; a picture of poise and calmness. His helicopter too had found it tough to land in the storm. But he came nevertheless, consoling all by saying that he would come again, for another occasion. After he left when we all sat down to after the hectic evening...we realised what a close encounter we had. All the "if" and "but" sprang up in our mind. This incident seemed to reinforce the sheer helplessness of Man.

Yet in all this, it was Man who actually triumphed. The victors were those silent people who like always merge into the background. Those people who is the real strength, the foundation, the cement that holds the indomitable spirit; the strength of spirit that gives the power to work selflessly. People so selfless, that I dare not take their names here lest I should undermine their greatness. Physically hurt, scarred and injured yet not defeated; they worked late into early morning. Their undying belief and faith stronger than ever, planning the next event; this time all set to outwit nature, with the indomitable human spirit of perseverance and resilience.

The Power Of Vote

Last few months have been hectic and in a way I have been caught in a time warp of sorts... settling into my new home, learning to tend to plants and above all learning to be a good neighbour; not my usual personality modelled carefully on the likes of my favourite actor Jack Nicholson.

These few months I almost ceased being a responsible citizen of India as I overlooked the inane editorials and the acceptance and denial game our government excels in. I believe that people living in metros lose out on the real India. Somewhere along, as they shuttle between home and place of work, with a weekend dedicated to a mall or a multiplex, they become largely insulated to an India where there are no roads, no hospitals, no schools... So, it is not surprising then to see young people in metros largely ignorant about the history, geography, civics etc. of their country called India. Hence it is fashionable for them to mock at politicians, some even dismiss the capability of a Chief Minister only because he has a name that is not easy to pronounce. Yes the "crown prince" is recognized easily after all he is "Cho chweet and vulnerable" no matter every time he opens his mouth one only gets to hear irresponsible mindless statements.

A couple of years back, I decided to stop being an arm chair critic and decided to plunge into the active politics. I started to campaign for a party. This was the very first time that I saw politicians close at work. I saw that most really take their position of being a people's representative very seriously. Every waking minute and hour of theirs was dedicated to people. There would be at any given time a lot of people waiting to discuss their problems with the person who represented them. The problems were of all kinds family, health, neighbour, law and order etc. The leaders actually heard them out, understood their perspective, and offered them a solution too. And in most situations they went back satisfied. So, here I was a novice, all charged up to reach out to the masses and make them responsible citizens.

I never missed an opportunity to educate people about "responsible democracy". One such incident left an indelible impression on my mind. I was at a jungle resort and the elections were scheduled for the next day. The care taker introduced me to the sarpanch of a village. This gentleman used to deliver milk in the rest house. He was there on a routine chore. I looked that him, he was anywhere between 50 to 70, wiry, thin; with sharp alert eyes. He was shabby, his clothes no longer white ... Well, and here is an opportunity to do my duty I thought. I reminded him that the elections were to be held the next day, that he must vote, that he must vote for the right party, that he must vote for the party I support as there was no way his lot can improve if he voted otherwise. All along he heard me, a little amused but showed no signs of comprehension. I wondered if he understood at all. So, just to check that my eloquence is not wasted, I paused and asked him "To baba aap kise vote karenge?"

He said "tumhe kyon bataein hum kise vote karenge!!!!!!!!!" I was stunned and stumped. That one sentence from him told me my place and proved his power; the power of the "vote". I realized that second that it is only pseudo people like me who dismiss the power of democracy and make statements like "we were better under British rule" The power of people and the triumph of democracy is there in the heart of India, that power lies with the multitudes who even if deprived of the basics still come with hope every five years to choose a mouth piece for their voice.

That the mouth piece decides to play its own tune is a different story!

Marriages And Anniversaries

Maybe age is making me reclusive or it could just be the latest Dalrymple that I am reading – "From the holy mountain". A recent social gathering really set me thinking …. "Am I socially challenged?" let me put my perspective of the evening which still lingers in my mind.

The occasion was the first anniversary of a young couple. Having spent just about 365 days in each other's company, the couple were understandably still very much in love. So, when my husband suggested that we wish them 49 more years of togetherness, the romantic in me protested most vociferously…. After all they were still in that very Bollywood *janam janam ka saath* mode and here we were with our experience and cruel practicality were measuring it down to a very countable 49 years!!!!!!

So, we walked in to a usual gathering where men, women and children had by force of habit segregated into different quarters. The men were as usual discussing and arguing about things that they can do nothing about. As the evening progresses and as the brews loosen their intellectual pretence and inhibition they all would come down to their baser instincts and discussions. This is something that I have noticed a number of times and a lot of my women friends agree with it too… Oh how much these men can talk! They are so full of themselves that they can go on and on each one proving that they are better than Alexander the Great.

The children as usual had been tamed with a loud cantankerous dvd to which they sat glued till nature with hunger and thirst gave them a respite from the jugglery of images on the screen. Quite often a more adventurous kid would emulate the animated violence and then there would be a flurry of activity where the mothers flew in protected their brood and told them to carry on watching the mindless violence "quietly".

Now the ladies! Well after having compared and consoled themselves with each other's turn out and jewellery and the uniqueness of their children, they turned to praising the snacks and exchanging recipes. Once this was done, the women were entertained to the dvd of the marriage that happened a year ago, as if they missed that earth shattering event! So I sat there watching a four and a half long episode. It began with series of strangers of various shapes and sizes walking in looking strangely elated. Then there was a shot of all those hungry guests as they were wolfing in the marriage feast looking appropriately coy when they became aware of the camera between huge mouthfuls. The educated groom of the event entered on a very tired and bored mare; almost symbolic of the life ahead. The groom was also accompanied by a whole lot of very happy dancing people.... The bride came in all dressed up unrecognizably and hideously made up. Then there were the usual rituals in the wee hours of morning where a very tired, sleepy and tearful bride went through the ceremonies with choice less dedication. For this real event there was no trace of the very happy and hungry guests. The only spectators were some very close relatives who just had to be there.

What was most intriguing was that the couple was rather immersed in the replay of this event and were even moved to tears seeing the bidaai.

With two boys.... I shudderrrrrrr to think of me being a part of this great Indian drama. But if the situation happens, then I will edit the video. I will pay the ultimate tribute to Balaji Telefilms by putting in scenes. Scenes like a long shot of me having loud thoughts like "Tu kya samajti hai... tu mere bete ko mujhse cheen legi?" "Ek baar ghar to aa kalmuhi, phir tujhe mein aise ghomaongi...." Etc etc etc.... then I will serialize it on the local TV channel. I am sure my boys and their brides will cooperate with me on this new business venture.

Boys.. hope you are listening!!!!

Of Human Bondage

What is the ingredient of nostalgia? What adds up to inerasable memories? I suppose it's nothing but PEOPLE. Good, bad or ugly it's the people who make the stuff called memories. It is the people you meet in the journey of life that makes you remember a place.

Recently I travelled back in time by three and a half years to a place where I spent six eventful years of my life. And everywhere I went I reached out for people. Some had changed some just the same, but I was bound to them by a bond which only humans can share. This bond is not a bond of blood. Blood certainly runs thicker than water and curdles very easily too. So, here I am talking of human bondage vis-a-vis human relationships made out of choice. I took great care not to miss any one but still I suppose there are a few....

I came to Jabalpur chucking very lucrative offers in Delhi... Like Robert Frost, I took the road less travelled and it made all the difference. But, when I left that place for Bangalore, I never thought that I would ever retrace the road, but I did for a fleeting three days and yes even that has made a difference.

Jabalpur welcomed me with its characteristic hospitality. My Ex- Boss was there at the station along with his sedan so that we could move about the town without any inconvenience. Can people perceive a relationship like this where I took the liberty to tell my Boss' wife, also a colleague that we would have lunch with them on the day of departure and also that we would like to have our dinner packed for the journey! Needless to say they were as usual more than expected in their hospitality and warmth. A lovely couple, more our children, who had suffered a recent unfortunate health crisis, but fought back, with extraordinary and praiseworthy resilience. Then there were the senior citizens group whose zest for life and fun can make any party animal to shame. They were as usual warm and loving even their homes had the familiar scent of "homecoming"! One had gone through what they call as a "Carburettor change" and the others who were still running their old machines were all ready to get the ones with changed body parts a new break in life in terms of a fresh matrimonial alliance in life! The toothless vegan senior, with uncanny semblance to the Asterix character codfix, truly relished chicken. The large hearted Sikh, who with his earthy humour and large heartedness kept all work aside to have lunch with us, Our "dada" and "boudi", who were hurt to see that we had not stayed with them. The classy couple, with their begging Daschund, a single, proud, father who kept himself immersed in political and social activities along with business. Then the handsome Thakur and his hyper Bengali wife who welcomed us with the same love and flirtatious affection Then there was this friend and his lovely family; all predictably idiotic to a fault, yet irresistibly adorable. What was best was that their daughter, glowing with pregnancy, gave us the ultimate joy of surprise, a grandson born within hours of meeting.

Some who had surrendered a little and had allowed the time to take its toll on them yet endearing and in all sincerity wishing us only good. Then there were our long standing neighbours who nurtured our plants like our relationship and proudly showed it to us. We visited our old home too, where every brick in the wall seemed to question our absence. Our long standing provision store where the owner used to share his anxiety over his son's poor academic performance and I would insist that the child would do well.... much to my coincidental prophecy the child actually displayed Sindhi Business acumen and had done so well in life. So, were many other students too... giving me the ultimate ego trip of saying "I told you so"

There were changes too.... little boys were on their way to be strapping young men... My friend and his four dogs had still not grown up. My colleagues gave me a mixed welcome. Some with warmth; others spoke a freezing tongue with icicles dripping from each word. Also my anti-social neighbour who had words loaded with sarcasm almost short of saying how relieved he is to have seen the last of us.

Three days of existence in nostalgia, till we boarded a train, to set off to the big impersonal metro. Even today, it is these people who form the major chunk of my conversations. My interactions with them have made me what I am.

Teaching me the ultimate value of human bondage, in the journey of life.

Kaisi Dilli Kaisi Shaan?

People tend to be loyal and partial to the place where they have spent their growing years. Maybe it has a lot to do with the travails of adulthood where familiar scents and sights of frequented nooks and corners hold a very special place in your heart.

As a Delhiite, I certainly have a very special place for the city in my heart. My weekends always began with a walk around Connaught Place. Friday evening, I would reach my mom's office at Barakhamba Rd and then we would start our journey with ogling at the latest designs of saris in **Kalpana**. A visit to Giggles was a must and then we would cut across to Shankar Market, where the best of dress materials were displayed tantalizingly. Occasionally, we would indulge then slip into the lane behind Shankar market where some of the best tailors used to work. **Nirulas** was also a favourite haunt where we would sample the latest flavours of ice cream and pastry only to claim that **Keventers** and **Wengers** were any day better. This was almost a weekly exercise that both my mom and I looked forward to. To me then, Delhi was the most beautiful city, the breath taking view of the power centre i.e. the Rashtrapati Bhawan and the North and the South block, the profusion of flowers during spring on traffic islands, the shady tree lined avenues of Lutyens Delhi....... Even the harsh weather had its bonuses.... summers had a distinct aroma of surahi ka paani, water melon and Dusseri mango, monsoons always smelt of roasted Bhutta, winters were a foodies delight with rich gaajar ka halwa, hot jalebis, khasta kachori etc etc.... My nostalgia would take painful dimensions when I would see Delhi in popular foodie shows and in movies.

My junoon for Delhi would be most explicitly expressive when somebody would have the audacity to make a negative comment about Delhi; a practise my husband revels in.......

But I must admit that in passing years my romance with this city has jaded a little. It has a lot to do with the rapid modernisation.... in terms of high rises, glass facade skyscrapers and of course the metro which has dwarfed the familiar land marks of apni dilli. What hurts me the most is the people.... after having lived a better part of my life south India that too Bangalore, I can't help but notice a certain harshness on the face of the people in Delhi. Maybe survival itself is a challenge in Delhi, where an average citizen not just battles the harsh weather, but also the corrupting fruits of the pulse or the power centre of the country. Though it is a city I grew with, I can't help the lurking feeling of insecurity as I watch hardened unsmiling faces all around me. The dramatics of survival has made the people put on an act to such an extent that their smile never reaches their eyes. The eyes look furtive and restless as if ready for some inevitable onslaught....

Today my Dilli looks every bit a ruin, my favourite haunt, Cannaught Place, is all mauled and pulled down for renovation, the unending network of the metro has made driving a nightmare and to crown it all the people, who swear and abuse for just about anything ....my heart almost says "kiski dilli kiski shaan?"

WAR

When you have a really smart teenager at home, make sure that you are armed to your teeth. Only here, weapons are different and the nature of warfare is deadlier than anything within the power of human creation, a war of wits and heart. And the war if always for the most traditional gain i.e. wealth. Here the parent feels that the lesson of thrift needs to be inculcated at any cost while the teenager all eager to be accepted among the peers sees splurging a sure shot to acceptance.

The battle lines for the monthly allowance is drawn the moment the teenager steps out of home. The emotionally charged moment as you drop a teenager into the protection of a hostel has all the potential fuel for a full-fledged emotional weapon arsenal for the teenager where a weakened parent surrenders as one volley seems to follow another. Here the oppressor is selfish to the core exploiting all that he can to suit his selfish ends. The range of attacks varies depending on the emotional strength of the teenager. These infiltrations are sometimes demanding, sometimes polite to a fault, a feigned illness or the most powerful the need to supplement an upward climb to an academic performance. Somewhere along, these pseudo psychologists have given this warfare a very sugar coated terms like "aligning to the world" etc.

I am hopeful that at some point in life I shall recall these emotional volleys with indulgence and will even be able to smile at all the words exchanged. But then as of now, it's harrowing and one wonders where the teenager has picked up such crass wily tricks from. Little does the teenager who is going through such a selfish phase in life, realise the toll it takes on the parents health. With age taking its toll the emotional whip is sometimes crippling..... when the threat is of going off food, the parent chokes on every morsel, then the threat comes in form of peer pressure by getting his girlfriend to put in a word, leaving the parent feeling deeply humiliated; then the threat can come in form of an injury or sickness where quick financial supplements are needed; then there is a threat that comes in form of selling a coveted and precious gift given by the parent; oh the list is endless.

I might have braced myself and decided an Israel like no surrender policy. But the fact is that for this hardened policy, I am no better. In this battle where my winning is directly related to my teenager's gain in life; where every step of success for me is a life lesson learned for a teenager; where every rewarding move makes the teenager only wiser but drains the parent leaving irreparable scars of life.

On Growing A Green Thumb

A well-deserved break from the grind and lo and behold I live today in a world without cares and all the time to just stop and stare......

The first thing I realised is the pure joy of working with your hands. It's no more the cursory cooking drudgery where one mechanically tosses in the ingredients out of habit. Here I am cleaning dusting even to try a hand at a repair and what is more.... "I am truly loving it!"

But the greatest learning has been from my plants that I have brought in to make a green oasis in my home. My son used to talk to the plants at home and had even named some of them; I had like a typical adult dismissed it as cute childish prattle. Today I stand corrected. Before I get started with what I have learned, let me describe my home. I stay on the top, 3rd floor. A home designed by a builder who builds out of passion. His sheer romance and involvement is reflected in the open spaces in the home. The home is open to all elements with a cute green garden patch. So, my pots have been fitted into all the balconies and an unusual entrance. The plants in the balcony are open to elements. What surprised me the most was the distinct character that each of my plants have.

To begin with the balcony with the garden. The plants here smile smugly in contentment. And pray, why not? They get the warmth of the rising sun, the bracing breeze and the music of the wind chime. When I give them the routine wash in the morning they all break into a dance nodding their heads, waving their arms about. And this smug, contented jive goes on all day. There are times when the breeze is a strong, but these plants never get deterred, they dance with reckless abandon as free the elements itself.

Now the second balcony. This balcony is open from three sides a little too exposed to the elements. The plants here have a timid mien. All day they grapple with the elements almost in a battle for survival. They need the support and prop that we give to help them face the onslaught of nature. So, here we have the true sons of soil, resilient and strong. When I tend them, they accept my attention with stoic faces almost telling me that they can really do without my extra help!

Now the entrance where the plants are completely protected from the elements and have an almost glass house kind of environment with a sun roof on top. So, even the light that comes in is filtered and eased in its intensity. So, here we have an assortment of plants which are by and large indoor plants. Of these there is one who is distinctly arrogant. When I spray water on this fellow, he almost smirks! And why not as he was bought for quite a price! There are two plants from underprivileged origins whom we adopted. These two are truly humble and grateful. When I water them they almost bow to me in gratitude. There are some spoilt brats who need your attention all the time. They cheer up when I am around and then they sulk when I move away, curling up their leaves in a grouch. The plants here are typically HS, all hoity too delicate to be exposed to elements.

Thus my days are spent in bliss with my dogs, my plants each with a character of their own, each communicating in their own distinct way.

Father And Sons

The saying goes that men will always be boys. So, I suppose that explains why my husband worldly wise and mature cannot still resist commando comics, Sudden, TinTin, Asterix and of course the old western classics. He boyishly plays with the remote flipping channels till he spots a vast expanse dotted with cacti and a solitary rider with the broad hat, the gun casually slung low on his hip with the cigarette dangling from his lips. In years I have memorised most of those movies and can even rattle their dialogues.

But then the boy in the man sometimes pushes itself a little too far. Like a kid he yearns for toys. One time it was a golf set. It was as if the absence of a good set came between him and his becoming a golf professional. Then it was a fishing rod. It still lies somewhere in the loft with its original wrapper intact. Then there are those numerous knives of various shapes and sizes. Some tucked away preciously; away from my reach as he feels that I am incapable of wielding a knife with the dignity that it deserves. He sulks when things don't go his way and the tantrums need to be seen to be believed. But the problem is this that he has gone way beyond the age where one can whack him on his bottom and chastise him for any of these eccentricities. What is maddening is he has an argument in place for everything complete with statistics and supporting evidences.

Yet... I am glad. Divine Providence exists. My elder son could not be an alter ego. But my young 18 year old brat is living up to his Dad. The youngster is as obstinate if not a step ahead. He breaks rules, lives life on his terms. His fads may vary but the obstinate streak along with an impeccable illogic to support all actions runs very strong.

Going by the popular saying that likes repel, every vacation of the youngster is replete with show downs where both obstinate kids refuse to see eye to eye on anything making it harrowing for me to strike some semblance of sane balance. No doubt, like always age and authority wins. But the fact is the two have their way and have their say, selfishly unconcerned about the impact on the other who is on the verge of a breakdown.

So, one continues to live in a constant state of emotional tension, torn between two obstinate kids dreading their inevitable encounters and show downs. My only solace being my elder reflection who even at a distance is such a soothing and calming presence!

What Next? St Barrack Obama?

I knew it! It was nothing more than a sneaky suspicion but now I KNOW! Nobel prizes are up for sale to be bought by the high and mighty, the powerful brokers of power who have the means and control in them to rewrite futures of nations. 7 months in office and here is a man who has earned (?) himself the most coveted award of the world! The Nobel Peace prize.

I have doubted the credentials of the Nobel Committee which had overlooked the likes of Leo Tolstoy and Gandhi but did not hesitate to felicitate Gorbachev for having overseen the breakup of the Soviet Union. How much of difference it made to human rights or world peace is yet to be seen, but one thing it did was to cruelly take away so many plots for Hollywood which relied so heavily on the cold war!

But Mr Barrack Obama, is the last straw! I wonder does the Nobel Committee have members of our Desi Congress in it? Maybe they thought that Obama would take a page out of Sonia's much crowed about renunciation?!!! On a hind sight, why was this award not given to Sonia Gandhi? C'mon, they could have constituted a new award for renunciation! Or better still the more dynastic patriarch, messiah of the masses, Karunanidhi, who has been on a forgiving spree to dreaded convicts waiting to face the hangman's noose. Or why not Shilpa Shetty of the Big Boss fame who very publicly and stoically refused to lose her dignity in the face of equally public racial remarks.

Now that all illusions have been cleared, I feel so much better! I can't help but compare the Nobel prize to the beauty pageants where indistinguishable beauties strut their stuff and then make grand, rehearsed hollow speeches on world peace. So, there goes the sanctity of the haloed "Nobel Prizes" The cynic in me cannot help but pat myself on the back like I did when Mother Teresa's successor Sister Nirmala in her very first address to the press after being pronounced the successor of the Nobel Laureate Mother said "we will be out of business if there is no poverty in India".

I suppose the best reaction to the new haloed image of Obama and the importance of Nobel Prizes came from none other than Obama's daughter who said "Daddy, you won the Nobel and it is (Obama's dog) Bo's birthday! Plus we have a three day weekend coming up!

Now all I am waiting for the fast track canonization; St Barrack Obama.

Sounds divine, doesn't it?

Austerity The New Fad!

The flavour of the week is austerity. It all began with a "scoop" that talked about two ministers who have chosen the 5 star comforts as against the humble (?) government accommodation. Such was the impact of the press coverage that it has touched all even the high and the mighty. But as an ordinary citizen I am a little worried about this austerity business. I must admit that my concern is rather selfish and might look very trivial in front of these great men and women who have taken a sudden fancy for austerity.

I am sure that there are many like me who have been held up on the road for an indefinite period of time because some VIP had chosen to use the road. My childhood memories are full of road blocks and diverted traffic all because a certain VIP had to be in some place in the vicinity to cut a ribbon, garland a statue or even a drive. The very "aam aadmi" who had put them in that position, become a bewildered victim of officialdom. But those days I suppose security was not such a grave concern. Politics had not yet taken the ugly hue of an ogress begetting uncontrolled off spring like terrorism.

Today the tables have turned. We the people of India have got used to give way to the politicians. The long trail white ambassadors complete with wailing sirens have become commonplace and most of us have learnt to take it in our stride. It does not shock us that our money is used to ferry these politicians to campaign and further their image. We have learnt to tolerate obnoxious spokes persons whose incredible arrogance (man-eating government) is very difficult to suffer. We have learnt to see celebrity advocates play with words with a snigger (persona non Grata for Modi) to add to the impact! There are also times when we share a sense of loss in a mishap but that too is partial to the celebrity with no mention to the other ordinary mortals who happened to be with the deceased VIP. But all this is acceptable..... But there were some spaces which I as an 'aam aadmi' had a right to...but even that is encroached now thanks to this new fad!

It seems the special people in the highest echelons of power have taken a fancy to travel by economy class! Oh no! Save us the horror! With their category of security! A recent travel by economy class by the center of power, had the paraphernalia called as an "entourage" occupied three rows of seats both sides!!!! Now the heir-in-waiting has connected with the aam aadmi by travelling by the AC chair car! The irritation was writ large on the faces of the co passengers who had to suffer the sycophancy and the security personnel in their otherwise private journey. However the star struck anchor person from a reputed channel went up to an extent of comparing this journey as a landmark in the ultimate connect of the dimpled prince with the aam admi. No thought, let alone a discussion is warranted to those people whose personal freedom has been invaded by this new found fad of austerity; no thought is wasted on those people who have lost seats in the aircraft and the train. What is worse the catering department of the Indian Railways went a step ahead to provide the Crown Prince with special cutlery and crockery!

I hope for the sake of the aam aadmi that this fancy dies a very early death.

As I watch the TV, I can hear and see the travails of an actress turned politician who went on a bullock cart to tour the flood hit areas. I must say I got some vicarious pleasure to see her petrified wailing as the cart almost overturned with her and her cronies.

Dreams And Drudgery

Action stations! Its home front now....but what the ****!!

I had dreamt of a well-deserved break from work; of stretching lazily in the morning and having the cuppa in the balcony facing the world hurrying by; I wanted to take a walk with my dogs and help them identify new territory. Speak to the wild flowers and chase a butterfly; Catch up with reading and movies on the television and welcome the sunset with incense sticks and the glow of the ethereal diya. I longed to sit in my own bar with a drink and a book; a quiet evening in my balcony with the music of the water gurgling in the swimming pool. Ahhh the wish list is endless small things but things that make life worth living.

I do wake up in the morning ....not to warm rays of sun filtered through my carefully matched curtains! But to a hurried routine of mundane chores so that I am all geared and ready to face the onslaught of the helping hands that have chosen to give finishing touches to the decor only after our arrival. They pour in one at a time, till they take charge of my home. Most of them need a lot of assistance in terms of suggestions, opinions, tools and sometimes even a choice of music. So I watch the confusion amidst the cacophony of their chatter and songs of Himesh Reshamiya. So, there you are in the midst of all this noise trying your best to not let go your sanity. Somehow they are all sundown people. They seem to be all attention and energy once it is evening when all you want is the sound of silence. They give you an incredulous glance when you demand that they stop their work in the evening and look all the more puzzled when you suggest that they could begin their work earlier in the morning.

Once they leave rather grudgingly, I am back to scrubbing out their footprints and make the home at least sleep worthy.

So, at the end of it all, it's the same old work and drudgery. All those dreams of wearing a flowing gown, with rocks glittering like stars, reclining on satin and feather cushions, smoking a long cigarette in a stylish holder while sipping champagne out of a rare crystal flute!!!!!

Ah! Such is the stuff dreams are made of!

Curtains!!!!!!!!!!!!!!

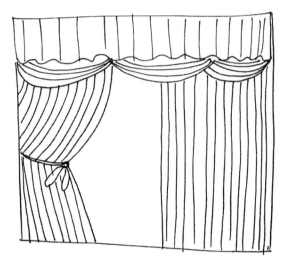

Its curtains again, for another phase of my life.

What do I call this phase? Corporate? No! I think "Learning" would be more appropriate. In this one year and three months ...I have indeed learnt a lot! These are some of my learnings:

- It is very tiring and also painful to be seated in a chair for almost nine hours a day!
- To make myself as comfortable as possible by tucking in each leg alternately even as I created content on correct posture in place of work.
- To keep my eyes and mind glued to the computer screen without even a few moments of a respite, blink.
- How synthetic the coffee from coffee machine tastes
- The glare of reflected light on the computer screen is blinding
- The therapeutic value of gossip especially if it is aimed at the bosses
- Bitching, works wonders for your mood

- Gesticulate through chat/words
- E mail as a strict "for the record" tool
- How not be afraid of computer jargon
- How to use jargon. to make simple ideas, look like rocket science.
- Complicate communication to display competence E.g. replace 'screen shot' with 'real estate'
- Make the best of a well- earned break from office
- Most pompous, important people are r full of gas
- One of the best ways to hide your ignorance is to throw an attitude
- Pretend to be busy all the time
- Your efficiency is directly proportional to the amount of time you spend in the office after working hours
- Be ready with assistance or solutions at the risk of being labelled as inefficient
- Being pricey means you are competent
- Boss has eyes and ears all over the office
- Never allow anybody else to set deadlines for you
- Boss comes in at the exact moment when you decide to stretch for a break
- HR is generally non- existent in any office
- "Leave" is a word that invokes most unexpected reactions from bosses
- A family environment in office means that you spend more time with the "family"
- Money ke liye ....kuch bhi karega
- Accounts dept people are as severe as the numbers
- Canned air is sickening
- Polluted air outside is a welcome change
- Even blossoms and a placid lake reflecting sunshine cannot take away the depression of a working Saturday.
- Even the Gods conspire with the Bosses by making special days like Holi and Diwali happen on a Sunday.

As of now, this is all that comes to my mind... I am sure you have a lot to add to these learnings!

Of International Schools

Namma Bengaluru has seen a lot of growth...... but for good or bad is debatable. There are huge glass facade structures, replacing the modest brick and mortar. That it is an ecological disaster considering the weather and the strain on air-conditioning is something nobody cares about. The car manufactures are locked in a cut throat competition while the roads get narrower with encroachments, and the furious digging competition between the BMC and the BSEB. Then there are those grotesque flyovers which swirl and whirl only to end up in a bottle neck. When one looks at these signs of debatable growth and modernity, can the breed of International Schools be far behind?

These 5 star set ups are the new status symbols in town. Your stand in society is determined by the school your child goes to. Many of these schools provide plush transport services but a more socially upward mobile parent will opt for a chauffeur driven comfort; naturally. These schools have a sprawling manicured complex, some even with a bizarre fortress like entrance. Naturally, in the portals of such an imposing monument, no parent would dare to squeak when a fee resembling a ransom is quoted. "Well hem.. ahem.... the syllabus?" a parent ventures to ask. Well, after charging the moon, will the school ever be naive enough to say ISC, CBSE,

IB etc? They have a customized syllabus if you please..... after all the business of education is all about aggressive unique branding. No parent gives even a remote thought to the fact that all these children will face the great leveller the Board Exams and then the competitive exams where a Surinder Singh Gond from a village in Chhattisgarh will beat the day lights out of these sanitised products of these international schools.

These international schools have such an outrageous system of education that it is a wonder how the parents take it all; literally lying down. To begin with they have no text books. They have assignments. The teachers who change every season, teach the students the content in class and the students HAVE to be attentive in class. It is imperative without a choice, that the child shall not day dream! If the child dared to dream.... well, its too bad.... as there are no text books to back up a slow learner. Oh, talking about slow learners, such schools have zero tolerance for slow learners. The hapless child and the parents are harassed alternatively as the "educators" pronounce the learner as a dunce.

Now comes the test- The eccentricity of these centers go completely berserk here. Tests are meant to test what the learner has understood and if the learner is able to apply what he has learnt in a given situation. Well here the strategy is entirely different. The tests challenge the learner as if asking "Oh! So, you think you know everything?" Hence a comprehension passage on parallel cinema written in an impressionist style is included in an evaluation for a learner in Grade 7. These 5 star breed of schools certainly are great admirers and followers of Macaulay the greatest villain produced to torture Indians. The students have to cram, cram and cram theories with no concern or care for its application.

This grade 7 child draws the structure of an atom in perfect circles to ensure cleanliness... elliptical orbit??? Hey what is that? They have some outlandish projects too where they have to read CIA reports as the nations they give for project work are rarely seen or discussed. All this fuss when they don't know the ward their school falls in or even if their school is in the north or south of Bangalore city. These schools stake their claim to fame by organizing trips to NASA when they may not know a word about ISRO or its achievements right in their backyard.

What enrages my sensibility as a teacher is that these institutions are not even remotely aware of learning Principles. The do not know to map a child's learning preferences or even their learning needs. I am sure that all these terms would be a jargon for the specimen teachers in international schools. Do they realize that if a specialist were to analyze their curriculum they would bite lower than dust as none of their lessons chalk out behavioral outcomes in their learners. And to add insult to injury, the parents who are the who is who of the society is quiet.

All their anger is aimed only at the inconvenience of traffic jams, the discomfort caused by a life sustaining shower, lack of foreign brands to shop and of course that irritating breed of servants who dare to ask for a hike of 500 rupees; to send their child to some municipality school! "What these people will do with education, I say" says the memsahib as she signs a cheque for her child's trip to the South Pole. "An interaction with Penguins" is what the pamphlet on the latest school trip said.

Raped And Draped

All along, the local News Channel, TV9 kept flashing this tag line "Raped and Draped". I happened to see this pop up while they were showing the Janmashtami Celebrations at the Hare Krishna Temple. I wondered if it had anything to do with the Raas Leela aspect of lord Krishna. But somehow the "raped" bit did not gel.

Then at 10.30 PM in a special edition of crime beat, the mystery of this term was revealed!

The story was about this convicted rapist who after serving 7 years in the prison came out and married the very girl he raped. The script writer for this episode had been so taken in by this grand gesture that the entire episode was shot with the panache of a typical tele serial. There were sickening images of an extremely happy looking bride, smiling ear to ear blushing bride- like, as she stood coyly near her rapist. I can understand the social stigma she is living through and maybe now she views her violation with indulgence... an errant manifestation of raging male testosterones. There were maddeningly idyllic shots of the two sitting on a bench in a park talking sweet nothings to each other. Strolling in a garden, a couple so much in love! Hand in hand with stars in their eyes for a long happy married life! The only thing missing was the two of them doing a well-choreographed dance!

So, the rapist raped her then draped her modesty with a mangalsutra and with "ek chutki bar sindoor" The cost for rape! The anchor was almost ecstatic, pouring out one wise saying after another painting the entire episode as a supreme example of marriage between divine repentance and divine forgiveness.

The entire episode was so obscenely ridiculous that I watched it in incredulous horror. In the words of Justice Krishna Iyer, rape is like a "Deathless shame". Its violence rips apart a victim physically, socially and emotionally. The wound of that violent act can never heal; a memory that maims the victim permanently. For the man it's nothing more than an act with no social sanction. And generally the attitude is: he is a man so a rape can be expected from him and now that he has done such a noble gesture ...C'mon don't hold that one mistake against him! He has agreed to marry the very girl whom he violated. Then lo and behold, the rapist is now "Pati Parmeshwar"!.

Will the cruelty of his act change or even lessen when the rapist and the victim become Man and Wife? Does the Parmeshwar now cease to be called a rapist? As a woman will she relive that horror and revulsion of the act again or is all forgiven now that it is socially sanctioned marital rape? No doubt, in India people look surprised when you discuss marital rape! Can rape be forgiven or vindicated by the act of marriage? Now he can continue to rape her and what is more no fear of conviction! Cheers!

Statuesque Blunders

My earliest memory of a statue rather three statues was that of the three ferocious soldiers in front of the Teen Murti Bhavan. There was a circular garden in the middle of which these three soldiers stood on a concrete platform. As children we clambered all over these soldiers who stood as a memorial to the Indian soldiers who had been martyred in the I World War. The well maintained garden around these statues was flanked by white concrete pillars joined by heavy low slung metal chains. Considering the extremities of weather in Delhi, this garden was a huge respite for people who lived in the vicinity. As children we played out our fancies too, quite often making the soldiers team members to ensure victory. Respect for the soldiers was the last thing on our minds; they were nothing more than sombre, toys taking on any role that we wished.

As a Delhi ite, and that too having lived most of the time in Lutyens Delhi, I have been surrounded by statues and memorials. I never realized the sacredness of antiquity as I played around the ruins of Purana qila, Vijay path was one beautiful track to race on a bicycle, Teen Murti Bhavan was the place where we rushed to drink chilled water. Rashtrapati Bhavan was a huge building which we always dreamed of crossing as a short cut to reach North Avenue from South Avenue It was routine for me to see new statues and memorials being erected and also the annual decoration of these statues. As age and time flew, I began to recognize the statues and their relevance. Too grown and self-conscious to clamber over them, my critical eye soon spotted many misnomers to the professed greatness of these statuesque blunders.

I noticed with dismay that these memorials are open to all the vagaries of nature. Quite often these statues became a perching point for the birds that sharpened their beaks on them and even crapped on them. Stories like the "Happy Prince" by Oscar Wilde only cemented my conviction about the futility of these statues. The saddest thing is that the people who these statues represent were full blooded men and women who lived life on their terms. To see them reduced to such a monumental absurdity is indeed an insult to their memory.

At this juncture, I do not wish to comment on Ms Mayawati's statuesque ambitions, maybe she needs to prove her larger than life status more to herself than anybody else. But the recent hullabaloo over Thiruvallavar's statue in Bangalore was something to think about. Such was the hype over the unveiling of the statue that it had the entire state administration in a tizzy. The Ulsoor road a day after this event is full of remains of garish posters, littered roads and of course a statue unveiled which like most of its ilk would soon become a comfortable perch for birds feeding on the litter and contaminated fish in Ulsoor lake. Thiruvallvar, the great visionary... did he ever foresee himself being reduced to a monument? To be helplessly felicitated by those who disregard the Thirukural day after day?

A Glimpse Of The Journey To Being A Major

The journey to adulthood, strictly on legal terms has not been an easy one. The emphasis on legality is only based on the truth that age and wisdom don't necessarily go hand in hand. A fact taken often as a bitter pill administered to me sometimes by the upstart, awkward teenager who has turned 18 today. I still remember the day he was born, Sunday, 4th August, 1991; at 1026 hrs he heralded his entry into the world with a full throated cry. The rains were delayed that year and on that day, it rained cats and dogs, giving everybody the much needed relief.

The dimpled bundle of joy puckered his face and let out a deafening wail the moment he was bundled into his mother's arms. That was the first time that a priority was made crystal clear to the parents: FOOD. Even as an infant he ate and slept waking up occasionally to thrill us with his dimpled smile. As he grew, he displayed a strong affinity for books. So, it was no wonder that he learnt to read long before he wrote the first letter of the alphabet. As time flew, we noticed that he has a distinct dislike for anything that was run of the mill. Whether it was music, movies or even the choice of books...he remained different and a non-conformist.

With a take and opinion on everything, he was surprisingly low key. He sticks to his convictions based on irrefutable logic yet he never deems it necessary to explain his stand to anyone. In a world that runs on a herd mentality, no doubt then, this attitude ran him into a lot of confrontations. Yet he stand up for what he feels is right irrespective of popular perceptions.

Deeply emotional, the persona displays "I am a rock, I am an island" as sung by Simon and Garfunkel. The only chinks in his armour are visible to his brother, and sometimes to me, his hapless confused mother. His father, his role model, is the only person he looks up to, is the only person he truly listens to.

Today he is 18, a big boy, responsible for his actions... as a mother, I have my fears for this unconventional prodigy. But like his brother says "Mom, wait and watch, my bro will be something, somebody, one day...."

Love, Loss And Lucre

The grandma sits staring blankly ahead, a withered album rests in her lap, bringing in more tears and memories of a childhood spent totally in her care. Now all that remains of her precious grandson are those lifeless pictures and memories which cannot be wished away..... Tears flow, the crowd of villagers pours in ....but her heart is empty ... all she feels is a painful vacuum. There is no hope in those old eyes ... nothing to look forward to .... She does not have to drag herself to the village telephone to hear the familiar voice He will not stride in anymore once a year like a prince opening his bag and handing out goodies for one and all in the village; the homecoming of her hero. Now no more puja festivities for her .... Just exist till she too takes the final journey...

The father lands at the airport dazed and shocked; completely incongruent with the airport's ambience in his not so immaculate workman attire. No he is not awestruck at the affluence... there are so many structures like this built by him in the city! He is a proud work man; a Raj Mistri; Proud of his skill, proud to be strengthened by a son who works as an office boy in a posh office in a big city. But today, he is poor. Struck and dazed by emotional poverty. The experience of the first flight does not scare him, the scornful looks and unkind tone of the manicured airlines staff and co passengers does not hurt his pride, the embarrassment of the confusion he gets into, over a routed flight.... all this is pushed into the background.... His arm, his strength, his very image is gone.... He will return to his village with his son packed in a small container .... a handful of ash...dust

The mother arrives...her first flight too. The eternally optimistic maternal hope tells her that her darling is safe. She was told "your son ...is in the hospital". She comes in an image of strength all set to fight any force natural and supernatural to save her son. She stares incredulously as the finality is disclosed... How can that be? She spoke to him a day before? They had made such elaborate plans for the pooja holidays... and now, this????....... The gruesome aspect of the reality is kept away from her till she sees the mutilated face. Crazed with grief, she cries aloud a series of questions to which there are no answers ....not yet.... Her only child, the apple of her eye is gone.. Her tears flow unchecked...it was she who had arranged this job for him ... why did she send her flesh and blood away to the arms of Death? Sorrow, finality and the guilt of the irreplaceable loss will sink in and live with her till she breathes her last....

The son has taken the last journey of his life. Came into the city and began his life as an honest hardworking young man. Endearing, cheerful, simple, always positive, he was there for everyone and anyone in the work place... Then why did he have to be killed so brutally? Why had it become necessary for someone to eliminate him? How could someone hate somebody so much? Wild speculations began to do rounds, too many tell-tale signs, he was not what we had thought of him to be, he was involved in something really dangerous and illegal......and so the ran the wild horses

The police finally cracked the case. The murders were friends, first time culprits. They did a recce first and then they returned armed with weapons, pissed drunk to rob and kill. Is greed so selfish that it blinds you? Is greed so myopic that you eliminate a life; a life that controlled so many other lives. In one stroke, in one hack the greed has taken away the consolation of a life .... Somewhere... someplace......where they could reach out and touch ....or even hear the familiar voice once a while ......a consolation that somebody lives for you miles and miles away.

Moon And Magic

"Young girl in Calcutta, barely eight years old
The flies that swarm the market place
Will see she won't grow old
But don't you know she saw it
On that July afternoon
That a Man named Armstrong
Walked upon the moon'

These are the lines sung by Lobo that very appropriately sums up the paradox of the "giant leap of mankind". I can't comment on the achievement made by man on unravelling one of the mysteries of the universe. But one thing I can vouch.... The day Armstrong walked upon the moon he killed romance.

Somehow, science and romance has always been at loggerheads. I know that there have been many studies about the moon. Scientists have screamed their lungs out, written reams and reams of theories to prove that moon is a cold mass that has no signs of life. Even the fact that moon does not have its own light did not deter a Raj Kapoor who told the moon "Dum bhar jo udhar mu phere" so that he could romance the winsome Nargis. And then Nargis complaining about the complicity of the moon and her feelings when she says "kyon aag si lagaa ke gum sum hai chandini"

Though the scientists did everything to break the romance of the moon through all their speculations and conjectures, they really could not make a dent in the romantic allure of the moon. The moon continued to be the ultimate companion for all those in love. For those in Love, moon was never a passive witness. It teased, cajoled, cried, lamented and even acted as link between lovers separated by destiny. Many a heroine in Bollywood took on the name "Chandini" only to add to their love worthiness.

But after that July afternoon when Man walked on the moon... he actually walked all over romance. Seeing is after all believing and after those pictures ..... The moon will no more "walk in beauty". No lines will talk about her as "one shade more or one shade less would have impaired the nameless grace". Why one can even drop the pronoun 'her' or "him" that animates the moon. It's a cold celestial body today, full of craters, hard rocks anything but beautiful and endearing. How tortured would all those romantics be who looked at the moon as a symbol of feminine perfection? Would Dev Anand's "khoya khoya chand" or Guru Dutt's "Chaudhvin ka chaand ho" sound the same after seeing images of o cold lifeless surface? The moon has always been hailed as a mute witness to lovers' longing. Somehow the moon was the perfect companion to the trials and tribulations of lovers as they pined for their beloved. Imagine how incensed would a girl be if she were to be compared to the moon! Maybe that is why our "eeeesh Aish" arrogantly dismisses her comparison to moon as "usme to daag hai"

Science has done its bit to explain many a natural phenomenon but they have never been able to create a dent in their romance. The theory of condensation and evaporation has not killed the magic of monsoons. Sawan ke jhoole and the thundering clouds still sing Malhaar. The tongue twisting botanical names have not snatched the vibrancy in spring. The very thought of basant fills you will colour and energy reflected in the vivid gulal. All theories of rotation and revolution have not taken the magic out of "jaadon ki narm dhoop" Any amount of central heating has not taken the warmth of winter sunshine. No amount of models selling air conditioners can create the magical languor of summer afternoons.

But alas Armstrongji has really played hell with our minds. Imagine... the very happening, bollywood endorsed Karva Chauth. Here is the wife all decked up like a jewellery shop, ignoring the hungry growls of her stomach, waiting for the moon to rise so that she can look at it through a sieve and pray for a husband or her husband, to be as beautiful and steadfast as the moon. So, as she glimpses the moon and then breaks her fast with the prayer; would she pray for a husband cold, impersonal and infertile like the moon!!!!!?????

Presentations And Personalities

Have you ever observed that some of the life style choices we make, distinctly reflect our personality? This struck me yesterday when I had to choose the shape of lamps to illuminate my new home. There was this Lamp guy, who flicked open his lap top and showed me various designs of lamps that he had. Well, I could see the disappointment grow on his face as I kept rejecting the fancy ones and chose the more sober and almost understated ones. The last straw was when he tried to hard sell chandeliers and he saw my husband and me completely aghast at even a suggestion of having anything even remotely that ornate and bling in our home. We told him "this is not us it does not match the people living in home" Evidently, he was not willing to buy that line after all in how many homes does one see a bedroom being converted into a lounge bar? We faced the same issue while doing up our interiors but mercifully we got a interior person who recognized just what we wanted and did a great job of our home. So, at the end of it we have burnt a large hole in our pockets but we are proud to have a home which seems almost custom built for us.

In the same way, I have noticed people's distinct behaviour on the basis of the vehicles and the colour of the vehicles they buy. For instance some vehicles that occupy more space on the road have a distinct largesse towards the smaller counterparts. While the smaller ones display an upstart behaviour by nosing their way into what little space they can find. The people who drive cars which are black or grey in colour display a certain calmness while the fiery reds and yellows have ants in their pants and given a chance are always the first to flaunt all traffic regulations. Whites and their kinds are the confused lot, as they live in fear of authority but in its absence show distinct errant tendencies. This may not be a rule as there are people who might end up with a particular colour either without a choice or out of influence.... In this situation one rubs the other leaving a distinct influence.

The same can be said of the choice of the paints and furniture in their homes. On one hand there is the garish display of loud colours and loud bright paintings and one can expect people living there to be dressed as a Christmas tree at any given time of the day. Then there are the subdued understated kinds where the entire house displays a simplicity which is reflected in the unostentatious people living there. I have a friend, whose house is choc- bloc with all kinds of curios and antiques, each piece with a distinct history. The person too is like his home, full of ideas and brimming with information....One has to be careful not to trip over something. Then there is this well off friend who has a home built in an acre and a half with a huge garden, swimming pool, etc. The home has the dimension of a resort, yet, everything in it right from the exquisite interior decor to the expensive curios, everything is warm and like a home, a perfect complement for the warm sweet people who live in it

Teacher Or Taught

Very often I have wondered ..... in so many years of my career as a teacher, did I teach or was I the taught?

Way back when I started teaching I remember a little girl telling me that when she grows up she wants to be a tree... because trees are green, beautiful and give shade to everyone. In her faltering nervous words I learnt timeless wisdom. Her words in one stroke struck down the routine "I want to be a doctor, engineer, astronaut, teacher, pilot, etc. That little 3 years something at that moment was the very epitome of intelligence.

After this transient stint with little children I was thrown in the midst of teenagers. Here too I learnt that beneath all their defiance there lay a vulnerable mind completely confused by the conflicts and paradoxes in the world. Yet they never lost their essential fairness. They would willingly walk the extra mile to help a class mate. No grudges, no preconceived notions just unconditional acceptance. I remember a boy who had almost turned an alcoholic due to some problems at home. The entire class stood rock steady with him and helped him sail through the crisis. While the staff had given up on him, the students proved everyone wrong when this boy cleared his board exams with flying colors. I have seen students fast with a Muslim hosteller only to give him company during the months of

Ramadan. If these students chanted the verses from Gita in true devotion, they also sang Sufi songs with the same ardent fervor.

The students were patriotic too and I learnt its true meaning from them. I can never forget an Indophile American who strayed into a schools one day and talked about the "dance of life in the eyes of a beggar in a railway station" and the "inexorable love in the eyes of an ill clad starving mother suckling her hungry baby" This American was silenced with one question "Are you romanticizing Indian Poverty?" their social awareness was displayed when they put uncomfortable questions to **Javed Akhtar** who very gracefully admitted that he is scared of the questions from the students. There were Television stars too who were asked about their social responsibility when they blatantly displayed multiple relationships, live in relationships, teenage sex etc.

I learnt the perfect example of team work and unity when I saw that any amount of coercion or threats could not bring out a squeak from the students. The spirit of fairness, when students en masse decided to ignore a teacher, due to her unfair treatment of a particular student; their deep commitment to a cause, where they would go out of the way, to bring a smile, or wipe a tear from the eyes of a needy. Their awesome range of creativity, when they threw open their minds to innovate and create.

I wonder why teachers feel that they are the ones who lead the students when it is actually the other way round... It is from them that I learnt to enjoy the feel of the first shower, the aroma of wet earth, the joy of winter sunshine and it is they who held my hand and introduced me to technology. It is from them that I learnt to recognize the distinct tremor, a prelude to tears, the meaning of a wayward flick of hair, the racing nervous doubts behind a well-rehearsed speech, the nervous cold sweat before an outstanding display. Oh I have learnt more than a life time worth from my students and my children..

No, I did not choose my teachers in school and nor did I choose my teachers in life. But tell you what..... I have been so damn lucky!

Dear Mr Kapil Sibal,

In one of your recent interviews I remember you recalled your school's experience as not a happy one. Sirjee, you were really lucky! You got something known as "school experience"! Today even that is a distant dream.... As an "aam aadmi" I cannot afford the luxury of schooling for my child! What is worse is your "aam aadmi" budget has kept aside a juicy chunk for higher education completely ignoring the state of primary and secondary education.

The nobility of education has as it is lost its lustre with gold digging businessmen turning to education as a lucrative profession. What saddens me Sir, is that you too have given good news bytes about schooling and then moved on to concentrate on the cash cow i.e. higher education. Sir, you and your government never miss an opportunity to tout your concern for the aam aadmi.. But where does this aam and not so aam admi go for an admission into a school? I don't mean those up market schools where students are taken for a joy /study trip to NASA.... Let's say a school with a structure with the necessary furniture and .... teachers? We dare not expect more than that as your esteemed attention is all on the corruption in Higher Institutions so how can primary education or even their existence catch your fancy?

I wonder why you never discuss about those International schools where children grow in a sanitized environment completely ignorant of "Bharat". Most of these schools stand on pillars of a certain snob value which is transmitted to the students in form of insane projects (the administration in Turkmenistan) and luxury cruises woven as an integral part of the curriculum. So, these students study various internationally recognized levels of education completely clueless about what Bharat is! I can challenge any achievers of these schools to explain the administrative structure of a district in Bharat. Yet these schools are doing a roaring business and have become a hot investment avenue for many of your ilk (politicians/ lawyers) too.

I am desperately on the look out for a school for my child. Most schools with a reputation(?) charge almost 1.5lakh PA. I know you will give me your characteristic scoff and say, "put your child in a regular school" Of course, sir! I have explored those options too. There are the Kendriya Vidyalayas, Bhavans, etc but unfortunately each of these schools come with the characteristic red tapisim and reservations; there is a preference given to Central Government employees... now please don't smirk and say "Why didn't you join Government service?!!!!!".

As a parent of a single child, I cannot think or even afford the luxury of another child. One is the financial constraint and the other the draconian laws of reservation due to which my child will not dare to dream of equal opportunity. The other day one of my colleagues told me that he has no plans to have children as it is not affordable any more.... I wonder could ....this have been a lurking thought behind an innovative method of population control?.

Chalk To Corporate

My third year into the "corporate" world...... and do I have any regrets?

Without a doubt "YES"

I never disliked teaching but teaching came to me without a choice and out of compulsion. There wasn't much of a choice... frequent transfers that too to remote areas ensured that I continue teaching. So, when we finally braked; stopped moving about in Bangalore, I decided to bid good bye to teaching forever. As somebody who believes in giving a 100% to whatever I do, I was passionate about teaching. I enjoyed interacting with energetic teenage minds which questioned and argued everything established. The only value they respected was strength of knowledge. The students were naturally fair and respected the timeless principles of truth, sincerity, love and commitment. Every batch was different, with fresh challenges. As a teacher, there was no rest; one had to constantly upgrade one's knowledge base to match the minds of the children. There was never a moment of boredom, only challenges, excitement and pure unadulterated fun.

Yet, I found teaching very stressful. My moods would rise and fall with that of the students and more than once I found myself taking their side in a conflict. All this left me emotionally drained and high strung. So, it was only natural then that the much touted cold professionalism of the corporate world was a welcome change.

I entered the corporate world and I was completely floored by the aura of the squeaky clean and quiet interiors, coffee vending machines, food courts, the complete absence of "Sir" and "Madam" in our interactions. It was so perfect. You did your bit and shut your mind along with the computer... no emotional baggage to carry home. The best was the complete absence of evaluations, parent-teacher meetings, report cards and the best of it all an assured tension free weekend! It was without a doubt PERFECT.

Third year .... Into this corporate world, I have now begun to doubt this perfection. Some of the things that I believed and taught all these years are now being proved false. I have understood that Honesty is not the best policy but what the boss says is. A rolling stone gathers hell of a lot of moss as he knows his worth and moves on. Behind all that first name based equality ...lay small people with dangerous egos. The survivor's mantra in the corporate world is "The Boss is always right" and "You scratch my back and I'll scratch yours" Dissention is to be read as disloyal. Dishonesty and word play are marketing strategies. Making mountains of molehill achievements and trumpeting a tiny doddering step as a giant leap in the corporate world is called a sales pitch.

So, before I sacrifice my principles that I taught and practiced to the profit driven corporate world, I really need to get back to my calling, to the challenges offered by bright intelligent minds waiting optimistically to take on the world.....

Written as a tribute to Mr BB Singh, the senior English teacher of Christ Church Boys' Senior Secondary School, Jabalpur, Madhya Pradesh

Individuals And Institutions

They say that an Individual cannot be above an Institution. Individuals come and go but the Institution stands a witness to the vibrant history and a promising future in its cyclic motion. Yet some individuals endure and become an exception and merge so much into the Institution that they cannot exist in isolation such individuals become the pillar on which the Institution stands and they become the jewel in the crown of the institution. They become so inseparable that the Institution and the Individual become synonymous merging into each other's personality.

One such persona is Mr. BB Singh. Think Christ Church and the image of Mr. BB Singh come into your mind. Any Christ Churchian, who passed out of the school before 2005, would have had the privilege of being taught by Mr. BB Singh. I had heard a lot about him long before I joined the school as Mr. Singh's colleague. My husband, an old boy still cherishes the Thesaurus that he bought as a student at the behest of Mr. Singh. So, Mr. Singh was in every sense a teacher-in-law for me.

Mr BB Singh taught English. Every bit the old school type, Sir used to be scandalized at the liberties that people took with language. I remember his shock on the customizing of English by Arundhati Roy in her Booker "God of small things". He could never understand how young people could say sentences like "it's the in thing" as his understanding of grammar clearly indicated that a preposition cannot be used as a subject/object of a sentence! But sir's personality went way beyond the subject that he taught. Unfairness, unethical, dishonesty were words absent in his dictionary of life. He survived against and amidst all odds, a symbol of timeless values and principles

Sir was always immaculately dressed. Dark trousers, buttoned up shirt and classic oxford pattern black shining shoes. In winters one saw a classic dark tie with a sober blazer. When Sir spoke to the boys about being well dressed, he was every bit the role model whom the boys followed blindly. Such was the awe inspiring adoration that he commanded that even the most notorious would listen and obey him in respectful humility. Any activity endorsed by Mr. Singh was a law which needed no enforcement. The students knew that Mr. Singh's wish is a command which they would without a question follow. Even the most mundane act would assume a stamp of sanctity if expressed by Mr. Singh.

Jabalpur, a small town was prone to rumours and sporadic chain of reactive violence. In such situations when political parties gave a call for a bandh it was expected that groups of miscreants would go from one institution to another and force it to shut down. When the Principal and Staff would cower in front of the mob, it was Mr. Singh who would step in and speak to them and as if by sheer magic they would disperse completely disarmed by his moral courage. Never the one to use an abusive word, he was a symbol of authority that students accepted and respected out of sheer respect and admiration. The Annual Athletic Meet or the Sports Day saw Sir in his elements. He would train the boys for the march past and drill year after year till each step was put with clockwork precision. The Sports Day went off without a hitch, synchronized to each second and minute. It was an annual event the whole city looked forward to.

Now that Mr Singh has retired .....from school and the world, the institution stands. The Institution is today mired in sleazy and cheap controversies. It has become a hotbed of bigotry and incompetence. It's pride, power and glory lost forever. A structure without a soul; without a conscience.

Nuances And Nicknames

Whether one takes it with a pinch of salt or pepper is truly open to individual wisdom or perception. But the fact remains that we all have certain peculiar quirks which is noticed by those who observe us. These quirks have given quite a few light moments which much to the touted rules of humour finds laughter in all these frailty induced quirks. Students in particular can be merciless when it comes to giving nick names to their teacher's kinky behaviour. The names are sometimes so appropriate that they stick to the person for many years to come sometimes threatening the existence of the very name that is their official identity.

In my school too we had "Sleeping Beauty" our chemistry teacher who slept through most classes. Then we had "Undation", the biology teacher who customized "Understand?" at the end of every point made in class. There were the harmless "Princi" for the principal and "Vichchu" for one Mr. Vishwanathan. It's quite possible that the relationship between the teacher and the taught had some remnants of sanctity which ensured that the names were not blatantly personal or cruel.

But when I began to teach, I saw a very different story. The students were merciless in giving nicknames. But one has to give it to them that the names were chosen with a lot of care and thought. In Christ Church Boys, I saw the most imaginative rechristening of teachers and though some were very cruel, one has to admit that the teachers deserved it.

There was a science teacher called "lappu" only because of the supreme laziness that the person displays. In complete contrast was another mercenary science teacher called "gullu". The students were eternally wary of the gullu- lappu combine as they could just about come up with any new way of making the students life miserable. There was another teacher who was called "beedi" because the boys got a distinct whiff of a certain brand of tobacco when they passed by him. There was the quintessential "bikhaari" also called "canter" who demanded gifts from students for all occasions. Then there was the dashing handsome teacher called "Banta" due to his expressive large eyes. The lady teachers were not spared from this onslaught. There was a lady teacher christened "mada gorilla" only due to her monumental build combined with a stern expression. There was this lady very liberal with make-up suitably christened "distemper" because the make -up could never survive the heat in the mid lands of India. Then there was the winsome pretty soft-spoken teacher about whom the boys would remark "video acha hai lekin audio nahi hai". A teacher with a quavering voice was called bakri.... Oh the list was endless

This was the way the boys overcame the oppressive tyranny of the school authorities. In their own way they broke the monotony by making the best of the little that they had. They were prevented from bringing a ball to the school to prevent accidents during the recess. So, in all their ingenuity they would wrap waste paper into a tight ball using it as a make shift ball. They would sing the Morning Prayer in rap style or set off deafening crackers in the toilet at the time the national anthem was to begin. Leave the class to drink water, then just vanish only to reappear the next day.

Such is the indomitable and creative spirit of the students.........

Antiquity And Anarchy

When you enter the portals of a school established in 1870, one naturally expects history. The damp and cool arches, the solid heavy wooden furniture, the grand old piano and high ceilings with solemn looking grey beards looking down upon the "bloody Indians" is to be expected. So, when I walked into Christ Church I was mentally prepared to experience a slice of history. Even the tree outside the main gate had a gory history. Colonel Sleeman of the Thughee fame used to conduct trials and hang the convicts on the tree then bury their notorious remains in the vicinity. The vicinity of Christ Church Boys Senior Secondary School Jabalpur. So, the spirit of the Thugs prevailed and it was no matter of surprise that the otherwise calm and angelic children would turn into absolute rogues in school only to switch off their devilishness once they stepped out of the gate.

The sad part of this legacy was the staff. They too had spent enough years in the school to be a part of antiquity and yes notoriety. What was objectionable that these men and women unleashed their incompetence and complexities on the poor unwitting children. The staff hid their callousness behind the shield of tradition and time tested discipline. Most of them felt threatened by smart students and even sank to the levels of being vindictive with them. Deserving students never made it to a position because the staff felt threatened by their sheer brilliance. There were some incompetent people who goaded students to join their coaching classes with assurance of good grades and marks in the practical examinations. There were some who would blatantly ask students for specific gifts both in cash and kind in return for marks. No, all were certainly not materialistic. There was one who attempted to convert students to Christianity with a missionary zeal. Then there were the traditionalists who beat students mercilessly and even abused them insultingly to ensure a subjugate superiority. It's an open secret today that the head boy, the house captains and the prefects are chosen purely on the basis of their ability to appease the powers that be in cash or kind. The matters have today sunk to such sad levels that they need to call the police to ensure that old boys do not create disturbance in their functions.

It is indeed a matter of shame that a school with such rich tradition and history has been actually vandalized by its own members of staff. The only redeeming feature is the boys, the students who in the face of all these odds emerge complete survivors and winners. In fact they see so much of unfairness and wrong practices at a young age that they step out of the school with all life lessons learned, prepared and ready for the world!

A Boys' School

A virtual multitude of close cropped head, in Khaki with a distinct green and yellow striped tie. I must say that the first sight of brawn was indeed a little unnerving. There was no trace of grace, manners, finesse or etiquettes, just raw masculine presence in various stages of maturity.

My schooling was in a convent and I was used to the hushed femininity of the building. The display boards filled choc-a-bloc with creativity added to the gaiety of the school. Even during recess all that one heard was girlish squeals and titter. Compared to that the all boys Christ Church Boys in Jabalpur was a real shocker. Come recess and the school was filled with boisterous shouts and laughter. Boys of all shapes and sizes ran around almost blindly like unguided missiles. And yes! The language they spoke when free from supervision was something that needs to be experienced to be believed. It was as if an entire herd of wild horses have been set free... The walls were stark and bare ... no artistic expression displayed anywhere. The Boys ensured that nothing even remotely indicative of stereotype feminine sensitivity came in the way of their macho spirit. So, all such expressions were torn down and replaced with crass, crude but hilarious graffiti.

However, it did not take me long to get over this initial shock. I got to know these little devils much better and was amazed at how simple and uncomplicated boys are. They are what they display with no hidden layers of complications. Nothing was a secret amongst them yet it was impossible to break them and get any information out of them. It was learning for me to see how easily they forgot and forgave. They would be involved in a blood thirsty fight one moment and the next moment one would see them share a snack like old friends. Sportsmanship and camaraderie were words certainly coined for the boy's gang. They are a team with differences within but to the outsider they stood rock strong with no chinks for the other to take advantage. There were occasional snitches that marred this unity but they were dealt with either the third degree treatment or complete ignominious abhorrence.

With such behavioral traits, the boys were a challenge to the staff that unfortunately could not live up to the students' obvious superiority. The contrast of the Boys vs. Staff was so pronounced that the management assumed an autocratic, tyrant mantle to tame their energy and imagination. As a staff member, I tried my bit and to this day I feel sorry that my bit was not enough.......

In six years when I moved out of Christ Church Boys, Jabalpur... I must say that I had become their fan. And what is more, in spite of the odds in form of the staff and management, the boys have done well.......they have become fine Men.

Dear Farooqi Sahib.......

I have the proud privilege of interacting with you in person. I doubt if you would remember me ...... I was a teacher (PGT English) with New Horizon, Nizamuddin. I recall that you were a member of the management of that institution. I vividly remember my interview where I was the sole non-Muslim candidate. I remember meeting some wonderful people during the interview with whom I discussed the power of Latin American literature, the romantic travelogues of Vikram Seth along with curriculum. My interview lasted an hour. I remember talking about the interview to my mother. I told her that it was the best interview I had faced and also that I doubt if I would get the job as I was the solitary non-Muslim candidate.

Well, I was wrong. I taught in New Horizon for almost a year after which I had to shift residence from Delhi.

In my tenure there, I did some innovations in teaching methodology which was endorsed readily by the management. You in particular were so open to new ideas that I could implement them and see the results materialize in front of me. I planned a farewell which was completely compered and conducted by the students; a history of sorts in the school. All these ventures were possible only because I had your support though you never expressed it explicitly. The greatest surprise came to me when Shuja-ud-din Siddiqui saheb offered me the Principal's post in the school. My loss, that I could not take it up....

Farooqi saheb, I have understood you as a person who is extremely professional, quality driven, and compassionate too. It's very difficult for me who has known you in person to see a rigid aspect of your personality which seems to be oblivious to a certain segment of people in the society. Your comments on Homosexuals after the recent judgement by the Supreme Court somehow smacks of a rigid fundamental attitude. I was surprised to see opportunistic, news byte hungry journalists corner you.

What was worse, is that they made you look almost Taliban like which I know you certainly are not.

Sir, I see you as a hope for the Muslims in India. Its only after such close interaction with some of the staff members there that I understood the richness of Muslim culture. I remember Wasim, the senior Urdu teacher explaining Ghalib to me, even today when I recall her rendering the couplets explaining its timeless essence..... I get goose pimples when I think of those words! It's on people like you and Siddiqui saheb that the onus of a progressive Muslim society rests. I understand your concern for the corroding social values which in turn is bound to affect the rich Islamic culture. I also understand the dangers of uncontrolled, unleashed freedom. But, please don't let yourself be threatened or cornered by personal beliefs.

In all humility may I see the Farooqi saheb that I had known? A true Muslim, who cannot be threatened by a handful of different people. A progressive Muslim who works towards a free society that should have acceptance and tolerance; the qualities that I saw in you and all the students and staff of New Horizon Public School.

Grandmoms And Rolemodels

Since I belong traditionally to a matriarchal family, it is natural that I see a role model in the women in my family. Though I admire my mother for her fierce spirit of independence I would without any doubts give the icon status to both my grandmothers. They both shared a name but were in complete contrast when it came to their temperament.

I consider my Mother's mom as the most beautiful woman that I have seen. Tall, dusky with chiselled features she would glow with both inner and outer beauty. She had the prettiest toothless smile which lit up every wrinkle on her face. Maybe terms like "unconditional love" was coined after God created people like her. She loved one and all. No matter how mean you have been to her, no matter how much you have hurt her, she merely loved. Married off at the age of 9, she saw the foundations of a typical matriarchal feudal family shake and crumble. A mini princess of sorts she stoically accepted the unfair division of her property by her own brother and without a thought served him with the same respectful love whenever he visited home. She was a store house of stories where facts and fiction would weave into each other taking all her grandchildren into an experience that lives with us to this day. She loved mangoes and one endearing image I have of her is sitting with a basket full of mangoes, surrounded by greedy grandchildren. Amidst that noisy quarrelsome cacophony she would dole out freshly cut portions of luscious mangoes to each of us equally. Even today when I shut my eyes and imagine I can almost smell her gentle sandalwood smell as we snuggled up to her pushing our fingers into her folds of flesh. Somehow we never got enough of her......

In almost ironic sharp contrast was my father's mother. Married to a very handsome man, she should have been a picture of poise and contentment. But alas, my grandfather turned out to be a typical indolent aristocrat, who could not even speak up for his family even during a crisis. So, my grand mom, exceptionally fair skinned, diminutive and reed thin took charge to ensure that her family survives. And she did a great job of it too.... She took all finance matters into her hands and dare anyone who could cheat her even by a penny! She was a terror where even a thief would not venture into her compound for the sheer fear of being caught by her. The lack of physical strength was compensated by sheer strength of heart, mind and oooh her words! She could put a sailor to shame with her swear words and the strongest of men would wilt in front of her onslaught. A go getter, she would break all rules and gets her way leaving people gasping with amazement. The only person she "loved" was her husband and all other relationships were for her only responsibilities which she fulfilled. Never would she pick a baby and baby talk to the baby. No soft words .... just business! Her diet was constant. No breakfast. Fish and rice for lunch. Fish and rice for dinner. The fish had to be really fresh or else the poor fishmonger would have to face her ire, over which most people preferred an inconspicuous death. Such was her power packed persona that all her children took after her, each emulating a bit of her but none even in her grandchildren could inherit the sheer objectivity and energy that she had.

Well, I see shades of both in me.... but I am glad that I have taken more after my fathers' mother. Yet there are times when I flounder from my objectivity and see myself being led by my heart which loves some people unconditionally.

Vegetarian Woes

Can you imagine what it feels like to be a solitary vegetarian among three carnivorous foodies???!!!! Though one prides oneself about being vociferous about ones choices, this is one place where all logic gets reduced to a stubborn whimper.

To begin with I am a vegetarian by choice. I was born into 'aromas' of meat and fish but some where my gene coding went all wrong and I turned a veggie only to hold back the retching I felt every time I saw a mutilated but decorated animal on a platter. I thought marriage would change my predicament.

But Alas! Love is blind. And I actually FELL head over heels with a die hard non vegetarian who felt that all four legged creations of the Almighty is meant for man's comfort and if possible the palate. I still did not give up. After all as a woman I do have a claim to posterity. So, when my son came into this world I consciously tried to create vegetarian thoughts action and food. But the aroma of the rich gravy(a camouflage for a version of cannibalism) did nothing to deter him from the perverse pleasures of eating flesh.

Try again was my motto when the second guy appeared. I must confess I wanted him to be a "her" going by the natural truth that women are wiser!!! But, Alas! the blind lady luck. Here I must confess I actually thought that I did the trick. For the first five years my son was a meditative young man who even refused eggs. So, I felt vindicated and I revelled in the triumph. But the symbol of my hope was corrupted one winter evening when the aroma of kebabs got better of his cultivated bias. So, now all three of them are at it in full gusto. I hear all jibes on my vegetarianism with a stoic silence. So, like the fox who complained of sour grapes my philosophy is "One animal cooked ensures many content bellies"!!!!

To Be Or Not To Be

To be late or not to be late that is the dilemma......... I am sure Hamlet would have begun his soliloquy like this had he been a part of the profit driven Corporate world.

I don't intend any comparisons, after all so much has changed ....

It's almost like a new recreated planet where the creator himself must be speechless at the race of technology where his own special creation i.e. Man is trying to keep pace with the devices that he has created! So, I accept that we live in very fast times where watching a stealthy sunrise through the clouds or watching a sunset flushing the skies with a blush would be nothing but a waste of time for most or even a piece of fiction. In the sanitized Air conditioned prisons where we work, sunrise and sunset is seen only as screen savers.

In these times, man has to compete with the machines that he has created. Anything that hints as imperfection is shunned as it has no machine like precision.

Who is a good child?

A good child is that one, who wakes in the morning, does his homework on time, studies to score at least 90%, obeys the parents, respects elders and here we have a perfect role model child.

And who is a good employee?

A good employee would be that who comes on time meets deadlines, never falls ill and yes works at the cost of his family.

Sounds impossible? Let's see what goes wrong?

To begin with any amount of automation cannot control the emotions. The same emotions which were the villain behind the first surrender to temptation when the first man threw all caution for a fruit, only to please his lady love!!!! So, any amount of automation cannot suppress that natural spontaneity which keeps threatening to break the method of automation. It can happen anytime anywhere. It can be triggered by anything at all. The culprit needn't all the time be attraction of sexes. It could be a memory of a wave, the feel of the sand slipping under your feet, the smell of earth after the first drizzle, it could be a placid lake or a torrential river, it could be the memory of cool breeze with a promise of a shower, it could be the fresh smell of jasmine as the flower girl holds it up tantalizingly, and it could be the limpid loving eyes of a dog. Oh! It could be just about anything.

So, there is no point trying to be a super computer. We are not designed to be like that, we are not programmed for automation. By living like that, you would merely be fighting Nature. So, relax take a deep breath and let go. Listen to your heart even if you need to regret it later...... At least you have a consolation that you have LIVED

Meghdoot

Intense, suffocating heat can drive anyone crazy....but very philosophically even this holds a promise...a promise of dark rumbling clouds full of thrilling rain drops! Somehow, there is something very romantic about the clouds. The moment I hear the clouds rumble, I am up on my feet and I want to be outdoors. No, a mere open window or even a partially covered balcony will not suffice. I need to be in the open ...under the sky. I don't feel the typical girlie fear for thunder or lightening, in fact I revel in the abandon with which nature roars and beats down on the parched earth...making her barren bosom green with life.

It shocks me to see children sitting indoors and not getting wet in the summer showers. I firmly believe that one must welcome the rain by stepping out in it ...by showing the clouds how happy we are that they have finally come. One must welcome the clouds like a long awaited guest. I feel that a befitting welcome would ensure adequate showers.

My earliest memories of rain are the sound of a steady downpour as I snuggled up to my grandma. That sound, that cozy warmth and that special grandma smell .....I am sure heaven, if I ever end up there, would certainly have a room like that. I remember bathing in our home's pond in a heavy downpour. I would float on the pond as the rain beat down on me. I would come out of the pond only after many warnings all wrinkled from being soaked too long. My cousins often dismissed my crazy obsession for rain as a typical reaction of a Delhiite, living in the extended vicinity of the Thar Desert.

Well, that was childhood. But even age has not dulled the craze for the rain. I remember my first visit to Mumbai. As I got off at Andheri Station, the urban squalor looked even uglier in the rain, but one look at the dancing sea in the rain seemed to make up for the concrete obscenity. I remember a sudden downpour in Leh, where the unexpected showers threatened to bring down the baked clay homes, built only to withstand snow and cold winds. A two wheeler is the best vehicle to enjoy rains. I remember being caught in a heavy downpour while traveling from Khandala to Mumbai, pulling up near a small wayside tea shop and eating the tastiest, steaming hot batata wada. Monsoons in Mumbai somehow seem to make up for the crass commercialization one sees otherwise. The rains in Mumbai made me spend an entire day, soaking wet on a bike, sightseeing! Another vivid memory I have is of a drive through the Seoni/ Mowgli jungles in rains. I pulled up near the jungle, stepped out to listen to the music of rain gushing through the Tiger jungles. To this day, on a warm and sticky summer afternoon, all that it takes is to shut my eyes and I can hear that music. The rain beating on the wide teak leaves, each and every stream dancing and singing in gay abandon as it gushes over stones and pebbles.

I know that I sound a hopeless romantic when I talk of my obsession with rain. Even at the cost of being Myopic; ignoring the furious and devastating aspect of rains, I still am hopelessly in love with Meghdoot who promises me some of the best moments of solitude, with the rhythm of the rain and the scent of fresh wet earth. Meghdoot promises me the long awaited showers. Showers full of caress; tender, urgent, and a little brazen......like the touch of a lover.

Twilight

Both my brother and I were almost militant and vociferous in our opinion that our mother's obsession with her independence is really a little too much almost bordering on selfishness. But she held on....obstinately. Delhi, a city where she had spent more than four decades of her life was where her heart lay. Any amount of arguments about the extremities of weather or people had no effect on her. Her existence revolved around the general trivia of life, paying bills on time, visiting the local temple, her regular walks and of course her long gossip sessions with her peers. Now, in this idyllic situation the only hitch was her age...at the age of 75, one really should not depend on the good health an essential bonus given to us by Nature or the Almighty.

So, the inevitable happened. My mother had a bad bout of an Asthma attack. She kept fooling herself and her children that she was fine and that it was just a bad cold which would go away, her friends too in no better state than her, saw it only as a routine ailment and they too joined hands in reassuring us that "All is well". At last when the panic button brought me to Delhi, I saw my mother on the bed, unable to utter a word, gasping for breath. It took five days of hospitalization, guilt of having caused so much inconvenience to her children, unconcerned relatives and helpless friends to make her shift residence to stay with me.

Today, she looks better- physically. But she is a mere shadow of herself. She looks lost. Her familiar world has suddenly been replaced and now she had to begin afresh all over. The sad part is the look of emptiness and helplessness in her eyes. It will take her some time to develop roots, a routine; relationships which will help her create her unique identity, her place in the sun.

I know this fate waits us all. Not all are lucky to be snatched away by the tyrant hands of death even while we are still independent. The very thought is scary, of being uprooted from your roots, of being thrown out of your orbit, to wander aimlessly in space among strange floating objects.

Bengal Club- A Love Story

To put it very literally, Bengal club was a shock too. As the cab turned from Russel street towards a portico with classic chandeliers, I stepped out of the cab into the late 18th century. Little did I realise that my jaw will remain in the dropped state for quite a while. I entered the warm wood panelled reception where we had to enter our particulars into a large leather bound register. I could see a computer tucked under the table rather apologetically for the convenience of billing. The receptionist, an elderly elegant lady, reached out for the brass bell to call the attendant and in impeccable English told him to escort us to our "chamber".

We climbed yet a few brass bordered steps to face a huge wooden chamber with a bust next to it. All along on the walls I could see pencil/ charcoal sketches of what Kolkotta looked like a few hundred years ago. The wooden chamber turned out to be an elevator, now powered by electricity but surely operated manually when it was originally commissioned. I stepped in and was surprised that the attendant would not use that particular elevator as it was only for the guests. There was another modern elevator again tucked away apologetically to cart all upstarts who did not want to be a part of history. I must say that every time the doors of the elevator would open there was a distinct sound of a chime a bell as if signalling the commencement of the journey.

Out of the lift and I walked the length of the corridor, with a tiled sloping roof supported by wooden beams. We stepped into the entrance to our room oops....chamber. Well the entrance was a narrow corridor which had a mini refrigerator again tucked under a wooden ledge, on the ledge was neatly arranged heavy spotless white crockery. A large door faced us and we opened it to enter our room. Since I am not very good in figures, rest assured that it was the largest room/chamber in terms of accommodation that I had seen. It had a seating area, a traditional dressing table and a traditional sliding writing table. There was a King size bed and a wooden almirah in the corner. The bathroom was just as large but with all modern amenities that one could dream of. As if this was not luxury enough there was a balcony to this room with cane furniture in it. This veranda was suitably shaded with traditional blinds which one could roll up to suitable heights to adjust the intensity of the rays of sun.

Our tea tray consisted of pure Darjeeling tea, a petite tea strainer, a petite milk container, sugar cubes and the exact size tea spoons. The tea pot was covered by an almost forgotten object of antiquity known as a "tea cosy". Naturally, the tea is accompanied with crunchy warm toast and bananas. We moved for breakfast to the "terrace" a cosy room with about six round tables. Here too there was a television and an ancient clock a mute witness to people who might have visited the "terrace" over years and ages.

The cobra bar welcomed the thirsty with its thick wood panelled door. A large well lit bar with classic round tables and a veranda with the wooden blinds looking into the bustling Russel street. Keeping in tune with modern sensitivities, there was a corner for non-smokers. I must mention a piano in the bar which is played on two days of a week without fail. Time itself would surrender and slow down to the classic charm of the cobra bar.... tempting one and all to savour and relish the environment with a "chota peg" where time has been trapped and captured to tease and titillate your senses slowly and gently.

The aromas from the dining hall beckoned me into another stately splendour. A huge pillared hall with imposing paintings and large comfortable furniture; dining here is an experience. This is no place for busy upstarts who "grab a bite" and "move on". Here one slowed down, would have a conversation, would relish food and the company you are in unhurriedly make those hours of luncheon last. As you savour each mouthful, one must sit back and allow the luxurious languor of the Bengal Club to seep in......making a Delhiite like me fall hopelessly, madly and head over heels in love with an experience called Kolkotta.

NRI - New Returned Indian

As an NRI ie New Returned Indian, there is no denial that I am glad to be back home. My Dog, my bed, my pillow even my loo is indeed welcoming. But somewhere the warmth and the euphoria of home coming get jaded as the reality that is India hits you squarely.

Please don't get me wrong....I am not the kind to be impressed by brands, malls and opulence. But, how much ever it might hurt my jingoistic patriotism; I must admit that as a Nation we have failed. Whatever achievement we see around, is more of things that have happened by default in the process of keeping afloat in survival. It is a shame that short sighted policies of successive governments have actually retarded the great India Enterprise from growth; a growth that can overtake the world.

My first experience begins with a grumpy Indian Government servant at the immigration. I wonder why these officials are not put through soft skills training, so much for their "atithi devo bhava" slogan! Is there a selection criterion that only people with unhappy childhoods i.e. people who do not know to smile are to be recruited in Government departments? In fact if you are polite to them, their suspicion doubles! Well, after the suspicious stares from His Highness Sarkari Babu, we are at last free to step out from the 'Largest democracy" in the world! The surprise begins with the very polite staff of Emirates, where on a mild complaint that the blanket provided during the journey was not fresh enough, one had profuse apologies and the head purser in fact requesting for an e mail id so that they can apologize to me in writing for the inconvenience! A change over at Dubai, well one has to put in super human control to keep your jaws from dropping. Besides the sheer extravagance of opulence what strikes one is the behaviour of the staff at the airport. To begin with the directions displayed are simple and very easy to follow and in case of any doubts, one does not need to search a help window. Most officials seem to know the area of activity very well. We reach Jordan. As we step out of the aerobridge and walk along the corridor in the terminal, we are surprised to see a travel representative holding a placard bearing your name, to welcome you. A country which sees tourism as a major economic activity, such a facility should be quite easy to the "atithi devo bhava" brigade to emulate.

After a shockingly cheerful emigration officer, who does not give you a feeling that you could be Bin Laden in disguise, one step into the crisp bracing air of Jordan. As the car races (speed limit 120km/hr). One sees that there is nobody honking on the roads and yes people who drive on those roads do not own the roads! They actually STOP for a pedestrian to cross! Though most people don't speak English, they go out of their way to make a foreigner comfortable they in fact look around for someone who can speak a spattering of English to help you out. Jordan is a country where you see people from different origins, yet they leave in tolerance and harmony. They are proud of the fact they have good education facilities so they study well and work very hard instead of waiting for "reservations". They are proud of their music and their rich heritage which is almost 90% non Islamic! We saw some memorable places, kept well and free of touts. But what is enduring is the people and their character, truly justified in being a proud to be a Jordanian!

Of Jordanian Bondage

When I talk of my visit to Jordan, I am sure an excellent search engine like Google will surely give my readers all the information they seek. Then let me share those experiences that were unique for me. To begin with I have to mention two people Thair and Saba. Thair, a Jordanian knew the country like the back of his hand but could speak no English. So, comes in Saba, a Palestinian, supposedly our English speaking guide who needed guidance from both the tourists and Thair. Thair.....in India would be Tahir....but Saba insisted that I pronounce it the way I have now spelt it. Saba, was a post graduate in Political Science from "the University". In my four days of interaction with her, she could not understand which university as Jordan has a lot of Universities. She was seeing Indians in flesh and blood for the first time. But was an ardent admirer of India- especially Amitabh Bachchan and Rishi Kapoor. One of her favourite movies being Amar Akbar Anthony. The mention of the much touted King Khan, drew a blank from her.

My husband dreaded the very idea of a question being put to her. A simple question put to her would need to be repeated thrice as her comprehension was clouded by her scarf and her basic knowledge of English. We realized soon that she was one of those typical University tagged people who never really learn anything in life. She was clueless about Amman, the town that she lived in! soon she became an interpreter as she tossed all our questions in Arabic to Thair and tried to reinvent an interpretation for us. Naturally, at the end of this exercise, we were all very tired! She was surprised that we Indians worship so many Gods and that we know about the Palestinian Liberation Organization, Israel etc. She began to look upon us as geniuses when we caught on some common used words in Hindi with Arabic origin. E.g Subah, Marhaba, Takreeban, Khalaas, Maqbara, Ajooba etc and our NCERT CBSE induced knowledge of World History. She was so confident about my expertise that in one of our destinations she took me aside removed her head scarf and asked me to suggest something to improve the texture of her hair! I suggested coconut oil and realised much to my horror that it would take me at least a couple of hours to describe a coconut! And I certainly would not describe it using gestures! But I suggested that she googles and finds an appropriate answer. While leaving, I gave both of them a gift and an invitation to visit India. They were very touched and Saba asked to pray to all the Indian Gods that she should get married soon.

Looking back on the four days that I spent with Thair and Saba, I remember them with so much fondness. The bond of humanity made Thair take me to a local old sweet maker where I tasted one of the yummiest sweet dishes one can dream of. They took us to a traditional Jordanian Restaurant where we sampled all their dishes including Mansaf. As he left us at the airport he promised that he would learn to speak English so that he can take care of Indian tourists. Ambika Soni ji, are you listening?

Oh Kolkotta! My First Impression....

Kolkotta......is an experience. Bitter and sweet, execrable and exotic, loathsome and lovable...

The moment you get off at the airport, the shabbiness of the entire town hits you. Somehow, one does not expect it at an international airport. It's not that I have not seen different airports. From a non-existent airport terminal at Leh in ladakh, where the pick-up vehicle drove right to the disembark steps; to the plush and award winning airport in Hyderabad and then of course the incredible, mini city airport at Kuala Lumpur! But then, Subhash Chandra Bose Airport, is appalling! From the cobweb covered roof to the stinking dripping rest rooms and the "oh so important Air India official" who walks into the security area even as the Airport Security personnel are trying to stop him. You step out of that almost 30 years behind environment into something that is 50 years behind. Rows and rows of dilapidated garish yellow ambassador cars are lined up for the convenience of the passengers who have just landed or I should say crash landed into the shock known as kolkotta.

I never thought that my first trip to the Eastern part of India would be such a shock; an irony in itself considering that my husband is a Bengali.

I decided to visit Dakhinehwar as it is close to the airport. I was certainly not surprised to see the filth all around Dakhineshwar as it is something so shamefully synonymous with Hindu Pilgrim centers. Though I must say that the idol of "ma" in Dakhineshwar is mesmerizing…no doubt Ramakrishna Paramahamsa could see the deity in flesh and blood. After a battle of a darshan, we decided to take a ferry along the Ganges to see Belur Math.

My first Ganga darshan and I confess I came back without touching the water even by mistake. I had heard a lot about pollution of Ganga but trust me, seeing is indeed believing; the dirt and the murky viscous water has to be actually seen to be believed! Like other things caught in a time wrap there were these boats scattered here and there in the Ganges, dipping in buckets and de silting the river. Belur math was a refreshing change from the rest of the filthy town. Here was a quiet and peaceful place where one could actually sit and meditate.

All along my drive to the Bengal Club where we stayed, I saw nothing but ruins and piles and piles of garbage dumps. I took it all in completely appalled as to how people can exist in dirt and squalor…..all this till I entered the historic haloed portals of the "Royal Bengal Club" if I may say so.

Enriching Life

Both my husband and I started our life rather late. At an age when most people were in the thick of their career we chose a laid back life almost in a state of inertia. It was a little difficult for somebody as restless as me to settle into a pastoral life style and I suppose it was my constant needling that triggered my husband into a state of motion. Looking back on the days thus spent, I have no regrets but I am glad that I moved on. I suppose that is why life is compared to a River. Motion or even a ripple being integral to its life.

Today I am quite happy that I am still a part of the rat race in the job market. It is consoling to note that you are still employable where my peers are almost on the threshold of retirement. I look at some of my senior peers and I am surprised to see how they have retired and surrendered refusing to even look let alone evolve to the changing world around them. I mention my senior peers specifically because I see a distinct dissatisfaction a disappointment towards a life wasted already. Quite often many of them are prone to a host of health problems more imagined than otherwise. They wallow in pathetic self-pity and suffer from acute persecution complex.

This is in a complete contrast to the generation before them. I never ever remember my grandfather or my grandmother looking bored! The men were actively involved in looking after the land and once they handed over the reins of the business of providing for the family to others, they were actively involved in the betterment of the society. The women ruled the hearth and the home with an iron hand. The pantry was managed with an iron hand making the abundance of harvest last and see the whole family through tough times. Once the women in control took a back seat, they supervised and trained the young women, occasionally showing their expertise in lip-smacking delicacies like pickles and other preserves. The fact is they led a fruitful life and were contented. They made themselves useful and never made others around feel guilty for their boredom.

The irony of the situation is that this state of sad self-indulgence is typical of the middle class or even the upper middle class. This is a very regrettable as the midnight generation has a distinct advantage over their parents. They are educated, travelled and exposed. Yet they have chosen to waste themselves. They are actually left nowhere. They have chosen to turn their back on the ways their parents kept themselves occupied. They want to measure up to the younger generation little realizing that they suffer from too much time while the working population is trying to pack more time into a 24 hour long day. So, there is a clash of expectations and aspirations leaving both angry and frustrated.

I know that some years from now, I too might be at the verge of this situation. To think that I can go back to making pickles and preserves is farfetched but certainly I will not make my children feel guilty for the state that I have chosen to be in. There is a wise saying that one has to seek one's happiness within oneself. I will surely keep myself gainfully occupied. Read stories to children teach in a school or teach in evening schools, participate in a community kitchen and if my body fails.......do what I really enjoy; write and reach out to people in the world.

Passion For Life

Passion....the very word evokes something carnal, something much wanted but to be avoided, something that is reserved for unabashed display or demand for love. But let us look a little beyond our tinted glasses and look at passion as a driving force. For once, think....what is life without passion?

Just take that passion out of your life and life becomes so commonplace so dull and routine. It could be something as mundane as washing clothes, tending the plants or even dusting the home...put some passion into it and lo and behold you actually put magic into what you do. The choice is not between the chores it is actually between the passion that you are capable of putting into it. When I decided to sit back at home....I realized that I loved every moment of it only because I was passionate about what I was doing. Now, I know it is very difficult to explain how one can put passion into watching a carpenter at work or watching the painter giving finishing touches to the wall paint...but yes a bit of change of mindset can surely make a tiresome chore more tolerable.

Now, I am sure it would appear rather far fetched to imagine that one can put passion into things as inanimate and unresponsive as brick and mortar. But here too I have an example to prove my point. There is this friend who is a "builder" by profession. And to keep his zest for life intact he decided to learn a completely alien language, dabbles in music, flying and now horse riding. Such is his passion and involvement that his flats, sorry homes are a complete sell out even before their foundation stone has been laid. Why? because what he builds is a true example of passion and like all emotional creations, one will chance upon certain eccentricities but what he builds leaves everyone absolutely spell bound. There is much thought and love that goes into the planning which is evident from the way he gives an ambience of space and exclusivity to every flat he builds. No doubt then, my home is in every sense an example of "neighbour's envy and owners pride". A lot has gone into the structure in terms of the interiors but one cannot deny the passion behind the original structure. The spaces, the ventilation, the light, everything speaks of his characteristic and distinct zest for life and the passion with which he treats all his ventures.

Much of what we attribute to the so called screen chemistry of actors is nothing but the passion with which the actors essay their roles. Even the likes of Britney Spears click only because of the passion they put into their performance. I am sure people of my age would recall how listening to Elvis made their skin shiver. Indeed what would A R Rahman be without his passion, would his notes be capable of making the listener skip a heart beat? Would Shekhar Kapoor's Bandit Queen have the same appeal without Nusrat Fateh Ali Khan's background score full of heartrending pathos?

Sons And Mentors

The popular saying goes.... "child is the father of man". But most parents are never able to cut the emotional umbilical cord. Some deftly use it to blackmail or threaten and make their children conform to their diktats. This unfortunately is the biggest setback of the human species. We never ever let go. Quite often parents impose on the lives of children only to meet some very dubious and regrettable considerations like, family tradition, and imagined social ostracism. In Malayalam, my mother tongue there is a classic saying to this effect which roughly translated means "It fun to see another's mother mad" Having faced the brunt of many such jibes overt and covert, I had decided never to impose such considerations on my boys. Yes there was a time when I needed to take a stand but even then the consideration was more of maturity and economic independence. But coming back to the popular saying...I firmly believe that parents have a lot to learn from children. As parents, we must leave behind our baggage of the duty demanded sacrifices that we had made or the supposed compromises that we had made to bring up our children. Worst of all, we must never use that as a meal ticket to ensure our redoubtable social/ economic status and position in the family which rarely ever appear when you really need them.

What set me thinking on these lines is a book that I bought recently on the advice of my son. Since I had a job offer of a school leader, at hand, he suggested that I read a book by Stephen Covey called "The leader in me" and as I began to read that amazing book, it revealed to me slowly how much I have begun to depend on my boys. This dependence is neither economic nor emotional, but yes when I want a tip in my career moves I do ask them. The elder one updates me on market trends and striking a balance between the financial and emotional satisfaction offered by the job. The younger one with his amazing analytical and reasoning ability offers me a solution that cannot be challenged for its pure logic and reason.

I must admit this change happened rather slowly. I have always compartmentalized my life. Though I appear to be very socially amicable, there are parts of me that only my immediate family i.e. my husband and my boys have access to. Maybe it started with my sharing every little detail with them and slowly I realized that they are much more objective than I am. More so my boys, maybe their wider exposure in terms of the young world around me give them that natural ability. I see them far more patient, balanced, and organized than me. At their age, I never knew if I was coming or going, but these boys know their minds so well even while getting into trouble they know how to take responsibility for their actions. Most of the time, the trouble happens when we as parents step in and take away their opportunity to learn from their choices in life.

To most parents letting go is difficult as it is born out of their concern for their children's' safety. But is it not crucial to let them go, not like giving a long rope, but to let them fly and reach new horizons? They must know that they are free from all fears to soar and explore after all aren't we there for them, an anchor, a haven where they can return triumphant or tired, vanquished or victorious in their adventure called life.

Family And Friends

Phew! That was a long tiring break of pampering, pandering, policing, picking on, poking etc. It started by my younger son who had become amazingly thin and really handsome arriving a week before schedule then it was followed by my elder shocker showman and then my NRI brother with his three Kazakh colleagues.

The home galvanized into action with the coming of my elder son. Forever a maverick, he came in charming all with his ways and the guitar which strummed many a heart strings. The younger one quiet till that time, stirred into action with his side splitting humor, mostly aimed at his elder brother whom he sees as an incarnate of Cacofonix of the Asterix fame. I cooked everyday to the insatiable appetite of my boys. The elder one had his fad diet and the younger one forever a junkie. The only point their food habits met were that both are strictly non-vegetarians. This break was indeed an experience. To begin with I learnt to suffer the scent of tobacco once again; I learnt taste for liquor can begin rather early in life. I learnt that losing weight highlights cute dimples and complimented with a good haircut can have really devastating effects. I experienced a fish spa and watched the hilarious "three idiots" with my boys. I explored a possible business opportunity with my elder son and am keeping my fingers crossed that it should work out.

My brother came in with three of his colleagues who were proud Kazakhs. At the threshold of middle age, these women really knew how to enjoy themselves. They were truly bindaas. Very accommodating and very unobtrusive, I really learnt a lot from them. To begin with I learnt to say "cheers" without a glass, I learnt that to connect with people all one needs is to hear each other's heart. I was amazed at their liveliness. They had no qualms about wearing a saree and visiting the local temple and offer tulsi to the deity. They shut their eyes and prayed in all sincerity proving once again that there is no religion greater than humanity. We had our typical girlie moments too where we discussed how men are like little children, the difficulty to get clothes that fit your special contours, the advantage and disadvantage of having curves and how important it is to be well endowed to wear a saree and look beautiful. When they went shopping, they were like excited teenagers going through a series of trial and rejections making my brother rush out for some life giving smoke. They were so much a part of everything that in spite of our differences in language, culture, appearances, I felt I had known them always.

On this Sunday morning when my younger son left, I was too caught up with work to even miss him. But in the evening when I hugged my brother and his friends as they drove off to the airport, I could not hold back my tears and I still feel a lump in my throat.

With Love- Mom

Dear Children,

Today you have inundated your mother with so many beautiful cards, thoughts, quotes and some of you might even have made the day special for her with a gift, flowers, a fine dine experience, a holiday, etc.

I thank you all on behalf of all mothers.

I also thank the market driven initiatives which have created a special day for mothers, fathers, friends, lovers, sisters etc.....lest we forget!

Which day can be better than this proclaimed "Mother's Day" to also think about your mother as a woman, a person.

There is much more to your mother; much more than that image of supreme, almost divine, a sacrificial woman who like the very Goddess with multiple hands multi-tasks attending to all the needs of the family.

In your mother perhaps there is a little girl who would like to feel the breeze in her hair and the tickle of the first drop of rain on her cheek. Perhaps she looks forward to lazy languorous afternoons when she can lie back listen to a melody and think of her first crush, perhaps she wants to hop skip and jump with her heart without being reminded that she is no more a girl, perhaps beneath her irritation and short fuse lies a woman who wants a little "me" time. It is so heart-breaking to see the perfect world of your imagination developing cracks streaking down to the foundation on which the edifice of her identity lies.

As children, you remain a child for your mother. So, you love, belittle, manipulate, demand and even ignore her when your whim demands it but do you see the hurt that you have caused that might never heal again? Do you see her as a human who has her whims too? All her "mood swings" are not connected to her menstrual cycle or menopause, it could just be that she is struggling to come to terms with her rising irrelevance in your life, the regret over the emptiness of her life.

As she tailors her life to suit your existence; there is a lot that she has to suppress, a lot that she has to give up. Would you not rather look and regard your mother as a person than this tokenism of one day?

In return for a life compromised and altered, is a day's remembrance enough?

With love

MOM

Monkeying Leader

Once upon a time, the inhabitants of the jungle decided that the Lion cannot be the King of the jungle by right. The other animals too are capable of Kingship. So, the Monkey was chosen as the King. Life carried on as usual in jungle till one day the lion attacked a lamb. The Sheep ran to the Monkey, the King and appealed for her child's life. The Monkey immediately rushed to rescue. While the monkey swung from branch to branch and shouted at the lion to let go the lamb, the Lion calmly devoured the lamb.

The enraged, heart-broken Sheep shouted at the Monkey, "What kind of a King are you, that you cannot do anything to save your subjects"

To this the Monkey replied, "How dare you say that I did nothing. I swung from branch to branch and almost broke my neck. I chattered loudly to scare the lion"

It is said that stories are a good way of conveying a message, learning.

Most organizations today are a jungle of sorts with Monkeys in leadership positions. They are harmless to other animals and they are reasonably friendly too. They work very hard, make a big show about it too.

But they are unable to identify the problem and address it effectively. In this situation, a clever Monkey as the King of the Jungle could have delegated the Elephants or even another pride to come to rescue of the lamb. What did the Monkey do here? Instead of delegating, the Monkey jumped into the field without the skills to combat the lion.

The King of the Jungle/ Organization, needs to be aware of its inherent characteristics and use it to strengthen the company. Here, the jungle, with its diverse inhabitants and genetically imbibed food habits, needed to come up with a plan to provide for the carnivores; instead caught off guard by the Sheep's plea, the Monkey literally made a monkey of itself.

Finally the classic heroic leader- here the leader works perhaps even more than the others in the organization. But, the catch is the hard work productive? The classic response of self-righteous leaders is the often heard refrain, "I work so hard, I meet so many people, I work 26 hours a day!

A Gurukul At Home

I watched in spell bound wonder as she did the *sthayee* to perfection with an embarrassed glance and smile at her mother when she missed a step. The best was yet to come – the *Abhinaya*. The exploits of Lord Krishna, the wonder child. Her expressions so real that the words "*Kede Chhanda Jane Lo Sahi*". flowed more on her face and movements than the song. The motley audience watched in stunned silence, the wonder of Lord Krishna, depicted by a wisp of a kid, all of 6 years, in casual clothes and a careless pony tail- Shrinika. Her face like a vibrant canvas played out a range of emotions – complicated emotions- *Pootana's* face in bliss of feeding Krishna slowly changing to terror, the indulgent anger and pride of *Yashoda*, the humbling of *Kaliaa*.... Watching this child perform was no lesser than a spiritual experience where, moved to tears, I could not even clap.

Shrinika, daughter of Sonalika and Shrimant. Sonalika started dancing in the Odissi dance form when she was in class-6 and continued her passion right through her Engineering degree. Her friends would tell her to take a break from her rehearsals during exams, but for Sonalika, dance released all tensions, so she continued with her routine dedicated to dance even during exams. The only time she stopped dancing was when she conceived Shrinika, but she listened to the music and watched Odissi performances. So, like *Abhimanyu*, Srinika learnt dance in her mother's womb. After Shrinika was born, two months later, Sonalika resumed her dance practice becoming an unwitting role model for her daughter.

Shrinika right from her embryonic age has been exposed to classical dance. Even the distraction used while feeding her was watching Odissi performances on television. She has grown on dance, classical music and mythology because like any other child her curiosity was on the movements and expressions that she saw. She is curious to know what story is being depicted. So, she learnt the rich Indian mythology even before she went to school. It is only after she turned five that she asked her mother to watch cartoon on television because she heard her friends speak about it. The *tapas* of having a dancer mother are evident in the fact that the child has never been exposed to unfettered freedom. Her time is distributed judiciously to play, study and rehearsal. She has been consciously kept away from junk food with occasional indulgences. Her mother is her guru and her father the pillar of support encouraging both of them to excel.

In other words, this child is in a Gurukul called home. Her different upbringing is evident when you notice her carefully among children. The first thing that strikes you is the perfect co-ordination in her body. On interacting with her we come across a confident child, sure of hersel, clear in expression. She displays a rare sensitivity and trust especially for elders. Another behaviour that stands out is lack of fear. She is ready to satisfy her curiosity without hindrances of untold fears.

Her mother wonders how long this will last. How long will her love for *classical Odissi* last as peer pressure in form of Bollywood and the likes of Honey Singh is bound to have its impact. Little does the concerned mother know that she has laid a strong foundation for her daughter. She has helped her daughter build a beautiful inner sanctuary; a sanctuary to protect her from any antagonistic influence. A child with perfection of movement; a child brought up on timeless knowledge and wisdom of sensitivity, positivism and righteousness is bound to be a happy and focused adult.

The Selfishness Of Goodness

Long ago while reading "the book of JOB" a part of the Old Testament, I found the entire suffering of JOB both exaggerated and glorified. Here was JOB who was afflicted by every suffering conceivable; physical and emotional, yet he would not curse GOD. What is the point; I wondered! I wondered at the way Man had been used by both Satan and God as an object of wager just to prove a point to each other. We have a parallel too in our mythology where Harishchandra, a King by birth, is put through all possible tragedies only to see the breaking point of his adherence to Honesty and Righteousness. What kept these people going? Why would they not rave and rant? Why didn't they just...Give Up?

It is said that people are like a mirror and they reflect what has been given to them in life. By that definition, both Job and Harishchandra are misfits and so are many others who fight all odds and still remain untouched by bitterness or rancour. Mind you, this is no resignation. This is total acceptance of slings and arrows of life but with a brave and happy face. Job and Harishchandra did not resign. They had taken a stand and that was what gave them the strength of suffering without cursing or compromising.

Sachu....a nick name, translated would mean the honest one. In fact I would prefer if he was called something more close to happiness, cheer or joy, but his surname shortened as is customary in the armed forces, stuck to him. So, for my convenience, I would like to believe that here is a person who is "honest" to his heart, a heart full of love, fun and cheer.

If stars could be blamed for things going all wrong in life, with no control whatsoever, then Sachu would easily qualify as a good example. He would look like one of those cursed children of destiny, who keeps suffering onslaught after onslaught. Born after many prayers and penances, he spent his childhood in a small town with a tyrannical mother. A break came in form of joining an arm of the defence services. Marriage was natural fallout of being an eligible bachelor yet it brought no peace or joy. After many a threatened attempts of suicide, the wife finally succumbed to a suicide bid and said a final goodbye to the world. But, in this bargain she took with her Sachu's human dignity and peace of mind. Legal battles between his removed father-in-law and him ensued till all people concerned ran out of will and steam. Ostracised by law and thereby the society he married once again. This time his life partner knew him like no other person on this earth does and was blessed with a lovely child. What seemed to be a typical "and they lived happily ever after" story, enters a new dramatis personae. The daughter from the first wife; as mercurial as her mother only much more manipulative....

In this entire vicissitudes, from childhood to an ebbing middle age, one factor remained constant. That is Sachu's warmth and love for ALL. I emphasise the "ALL" because that is what has kept him going. We all have our own shields, our own self defence mechanism that protects us from the unfairness of the world. For Sachu, his self defence mechanism is loving and caring for people unconditionally. Great guy; isn't it?

Well, one hears conflicting and contrary reactions. For most, he is a great friend and every bit a friend in need. But, such people are Islands. They hear and heed only their inner call and are almost insensitively deaf or immune to anything contrary. His goodness is for all and anybody. Like a whiff of refreshing breeze he is here one moment and then gone. He cannot be captured or confined in relationships or spaces. The one who tries to capture his essence or even stake a claim on it is in for a rude shock. It is an ironic polarity; goodness and selfishness.

And so he continues to LIVE on his terms and by his rules. As he organized another gathering of his friends, he moved among the people, taking care of all, looking into every nuance, looking into every detail, making sure that all guests feel welcomed and cared for; including his wife As we parted late in the evening, he saw off every guest, and the next day, Facebook was inundated with praises. But, does he care? I doubt. It is an inner urge that he is satisfying, his defence mechanism against the pettiness, ugliness and tears that life has meted out to him.

How dare You.......you woman!!!!!

There is no statistical data to show the double standards Indians practice so blatantly and so proudly.

This can be seen most blatantly in the trolling that has happened after the recent cabinet reshuffle. The solitary Lady Minister has already faced enough flak after she was appointed as the HRD Ministry. She was just about stripped of all dignity except the physical variety for the fear of legal ramifications. Her spirited and feisty personality only added fuel to fire. Now the reshuffle has invited a fresh flood of snide and sexist remarks.

Humour is an inherent part of a vibrant democracy. I remember a post on facebook, after Modi's speech in the US Congress:

"Modi ji ki speech sunkar US ne bola..

Na Trump chahiye na hi Hillary.

Abki baar Modi Sarkar"

There is a very subtle dividing line between humour and comments and pictures that smack of gender bias and gender stereotypes which are definitely not funny. For example the image that is almost viral on twitter with multiple shares, likes and comments.

What is shocking is that the trolling is done by both men and women.

What makes this particular lady minister a butt of so much trolling? Is it her successful and almost iconic stint of a lady protagonist in a popular soap? Is it that she has the gift of the gab and can take any veteran politician on the floor of the house or in public? Is it her efficiency and success in plunging into a work assigned to her?

All the reactions are nothing but sheer jealousy of both men and women towards a woman who has made her life into a success story through sheer hard work and determination. Why is it so difficult for both men and women to acknowledge a woman who has made it in life? Most men irrespective of their education or economic status are intimidated by strong and successful women. But, why do women turn against one of their sisters who have taken challenges head on? Why do they do everything in their power to drag her down to the mediocrity that they are wallowing in; a mediocrity they detest and hate?

So, ladies and gentlemen, instead of being like the classic RIN tag line "bhala uski kameez meri kameez say safed kaise?" Applaud and appreciate the fact that we have women like Ms Jayalaitha, Ms Mamta Bannerji, Ms Mayawati, Ms Sushma Swaraj, Ms Mehbooba Mufti and Ms Smriti Irani. These women have broken into gender bastions and in their own way have opened avenues for other women and an opportunity for men to gulp their egos.

The Sour Grapes

Ammu had waited eagerly for the monsoons to end, she could now go to the school near her father's home. Her mother's home was bigger but she loved the cosy warmth of her father's home tucked away securely under a huge rock. But, come rains, her father's home would be cut off as the fields would get flooded. She would climb the rock with the other siblings and cousins, stop to catch her breath on top of the rock, take in the view of the vast expanse of shades of green; bright, dark and deep dark. Then she would race down to the school. She was the smart one in the class, so the moment she entered the class, she was given the responsibility of putting the table for the teacher in order. She dusted the table with her hands, placed the cane with reverence and four pieces of chalk neatly on the table.

Today was special; there was a new teacher today. He had just passed the ESLC – Elementary School leaving Certificate examination and had to teach for 6 months in this school before he goes to be trained as a teacher. She made sure that everything was in order and then went to her place. She checked her books, Malayalam, Maths, Social Studies and Civics. All in order.

In fact she loved everything about this school, the village, her father's home. She loved tucking up to her father in the evening listening to his soothing voice, she loved exploring the land, picking up a coconut here, checking the readiness of a jackfruit, counting the mangoes on the tree and above all playing "trump" with her father and mother in the evening, watching long serious shadows in the dim lamp light. Then came the rains, flooding everything, water breaching the canal walls till the field and canal looked like one river in a big hurry. Ammu and her brother would get to work, make a makeshift raft and row into the flow, retrieving a bunch of bananas, a wandering log, lost coconuts, anything that the water had taken along on its perennial journey. All this continued till the water levels grew and it was time to relocate.

Relocation to Ammu's ancestral home; her mother's home- her real home. Her home- large and dry; dry of fun, dry of warmth. In the home teeming with aunts, uncles and their helping hands, smoke filled kitchen fires that never went out, a home that beat the residential rooster in the morning and worked till the moon said goodbye in the horizon. In this large home, space was always short. Space to sleep; space to rest; space to idle; space to dream; space in people's hearts.

Ammu learnt the first letters of the Malayalam alphabet in her maternal home. She remembers getting the shell of a tender coconut ready. After scraping the inside of the coconut, she washed and dried it. Then she filled it with sand and used a paper to plug the hole. This was what she carried to the Kalari; a make shift shed where a teacher would teach the children the letters of the Malayalam alphabet on the sand that each student carried in their tender coconut. This was a school only meant for her family, no outsider could dare to be a part of this exclusive learning. Her elder sisters and aunts who had never seen a school had studied in a Kalari and were voracious readers, their favourite being Raghuvamsham.

Ammu would wait anxiously for --------------------the day the monsoons officially ended and she would race to her father's home. There she went to a school, full of laughing and running children. She stood in an assembly, said the prayers and had so many friends. She also had real books to read and write. And Ammu was a bright girl, a pet of all her teachers. So, Ammu was the monitor and she had to make sure that everything was ready for the new teacher.

The new teacher came wearing a spotless white mundu and a white shirt. He looked around furtively at the students and asked them all to sit down. His hands shook as he picked a chalk up to write and cleared his throat several times. Then he told them the story of the Fox trying to reach the grapes. Everybody had heard the story, but no one said a word and listened to the teacher with rapt attention; more attentive to the teacher's nervous gestures than the story. Now that the story was over, the teacher looked around the class, not knowing what to do. Then an idea struck him. He called the students one by one and held up the stick and asked them to be like the fox and jump up to bite the stick. Every time a child reached close to the stick, the teacher raised the stick. Ammu too watched eagerly, but could not understand how a bunch of grapes can move up. When it was her turn, she refused to jump. "WHAT?????? WHY????" screamed the teacher. "Because Sir, grapes can't move up and if you don't move the grapes we would have caught it long ago"

The teacher trembled with anger and stared at the wisp of a girl who had challenged his authority. He held her hands out and rapped hard on each knuckle. Ammu cried out in both pain and shame of censure. What wrong had she done?

The next day she came to school, red eyed and running nose. She held on to her father's hand and entered the school looking here and there for the new teacher. The Principal stood up to greet her father as they were friends. But, Ammu's father was livid. He showed the sore knuckle to the Principal and asked him what kind of teachers he had appointed in the school? The Principal was shocked too; he asked Ammu why she was beaten. She said "I could not reach the grapes and sir became angry" The Principal reassured Ammu's father and Ammu's father left with the usual threat of taking the child out of the school.

Her marriage liberated her, taking her to distant lands, meeting different people. With the support of her husband she began to work. Yet she never forgot the sour grapes.

These grapes kept coming back to her. Her denied further education, a permission not given to her to work, a marriage that brought with it sacrifices for the newly acquired family, her office where she saw manipulations for small victories, her new city friends about whom she was never sure, her children who never seemed to have time for her, poor health and dependence.....sour grapes, sour grapes and sour grapes, all along with no indulgent father to protect her and warn them all away.

When Education Fails

Rohan Imtiaz, Shamim Mubashir and Nibras Islam...can't get over the faces of these boys. They have the same freshness of hope, smiles with traces of childishness....and these boys turned killers. Gunning down people who were non -muslims, who could not recite from the Quran, who were not wearing a hijab.

These boys look so much like the boys I have taught. These boys could have been in my classroom, learning Shakespeare and Shelly with me.... and to think that any of my students due to some quirk can become killers?

While the media goes overboard in getting better of each other in obtaining more and more gory details; I am yet to see even one article that looks into why these boys chose this path. What made these boys who chose to kill and then become Martyrs to have the glory of Jannat?

Off late, the newspapers are full of reports of juvenile offenders; offenders who seem to outdo the wildest imagination of cruelty. But, how many voices do we hear that probes or demands a probe that looks into the cause for such ugly contortions and convolutions in behaviour?

We all mirror what we see and perceive. Right from the playschool, where today urban parents enrol children even before they have been weaned, to the Primary level of schooling, a child is subjected to so many influences, family, society, school, peers etc.

Of all these influencers, the school has maximum responsibility.

Schools are today factories churning out perfect products on the assembly line. Any aberration is rejected and thrown away as junk. Zero tolerance for imperfection or innovation; a system inspired by Industrial Revolution, with the sole objective of creating perfect machines. What we have forgotten in creating more and more players in the rat race is that human beings are emotional and sensual and highly individualistic creatures and an existence of mechanical perfection can only cause breakdowns.

What if our schools and the education system had just one objective i.e. pursue happiness? If only the schools taught students to recognize what makes them happy. Now I know that this sounds Utopian but I am sure that schools till class 2 can surely focus on this. Once children pursue happiness, they will automatically learn values of humanity: love, tolerance, compassion, etc. Children with their inherent sense of fairness, free from adult imposed pressures will learn to be in touch with their core feelings and recognize that what makes them happy is something universal and free from boundaries of power, pelf and prejudices. No doubt he schools will have to focus on teachers teaching in playschools, nurseries and kindergarten. They will have to redesign curriculum and most important have an evaluation system where a child's positive traits are highlighted against marks which are more of a report card on successful regimentation. In a society with so many disparities it is only the school, the education system that an prevent this ticking bomb from going off.

Considering the troubled times today, considering that young people from a reasonably well to do background are turning to violence, considering that students have begun to seek martyrdom and glory in violence and death, it will be surely worth a discussion and a try, to change a failed education system, the only hope at the end of the dark tunnel. Are the NDTVs, CNN IBN, Times Now, etc. listening?

Printed in the United States
By Bookmasters